SENECA

PHAEDRA

MASTERS OF LATIN LITERATURE

EDITORS: FREDERICK AHL, DISKIN CLAY,
DOUGLASS PARKER, JON STALLWORTHY

This series aims to help reestablish the importance and intrinsic interest of Latin literature in an age which has rejected the Latin literary model in favor of the Greek. We plan to make available, in modern English-language versions, influential Latin works, especially poetry, from the third century B.C. to the eighteenth century of our own era. By "influential works" we mean not only those commonly read in the classroom today, either in the original or in translation, but also those which shaped literature in their own and in subsequent times, yet have now either lost or been dismissed from their places among the "Great Books" of our culture.

SENECA

PHAEDRA

TRANSLATED AND WITH

AN INTRODUCTION BY

FREDERICK AHL

Cornell University Press

ITHACA AND LONDON

First published 1986 by Cornell University Press.
First printing, Cornell Paperbacks, 1986.
Third printing 1994.

International Standard Book Number 0-8014-9433-8
Library of Congress Catalog Card Number 86-47634
Printed in the United States of America
*Librarians: Library of Congress cataloging information
appears on the last page of the book.*

To the memory of Kathleen Mary Cain Ahl

Ní chuala mé in aird sa bhith
ceol ba binne ná do cheol
agus tú fá bhun do nid

Contents

General Introduction

Seneca's Life

Lucius Annaeus Seneca was born in Córdoba, Spain, shortly before the traditional date for the birth of Christ, around 1 B.C., to a family famous and influential in both politics and literature. He was the son of another Lucius Annaeus Seneca (the "Elder"), some of whose works, the *Controversiae* or *Exercises in Persuasion*, survive. His brother, Annaeus Mela, was father of the poet Lucan (Marcus Annaeus Lucanus), author of the *Pharsalia*, an epic poem which tells of the civil wars between Julius Caesar and his military and ideological opponents. Another brother, Lucius Iunius Novatus Gallio (so named because he was adopted by Iunius Gallio), is mentioned in Acts 18:12–18 as the proconsular governor of Achaea in Greece who refused to hear the Jews' case against Paul.

Early Christian writers were aware that the founders of Christianity and the famous philosophical and political family of Seneca were contemporaries. Tertullian describes Seneca as "often one of us,"[1] and there even survives a forged correspondence between Seneca and Paul, full of mutual praise in rather awkward Latin.[2] People found it hard to believe that the world of the Annaei and that of the Christian missionary, which touched in so many ways, should not have pro-

---

[1] *On the Soul* 20.

[2] C. W. Barlow, ed., *Epistolae Senecae ad Paulum et Pauli ad Senecam (Quae Vocantur)* (New York, 1938). Despite the forbidding title, the text is both in Latin and in English translation.

9

duced literary contact, especially since Paul and Seneca both fell victim to the emperor Nero. Paul and, traditionally, other disciples were put to death by Nero during his purge of the Christians in the aftermath of the great fire at Rome (A.D. 64). Similarly, Seneca and members of his family— Gallio, Mela, and Lucan—were all suspected of involvement in a plot to kill Nero the year after the fire (A.D. 65) and obliged to commit suicide.

Although Seneca, like many intellectuals of the first and second centuries A.D. (including his severest ancient critic, the rhetorician Quintilian), was of Spanish origin, he spent most of his life at Rome under the Julio-Claudian imperial dynasty. He was born in Augustus' reign, held his first major political office under Tiberius (A.D. 33), and was a famous orator by the time Caligula succeeded to the throne (A.D. 37). Although his success apparently excited Caligula's jealousy, it was not until the first year of Claudius' reign (A.D. 41) that Seneca first experienced the force of imperial displeasure. He incurred the wrath of Claudius' wife, Messalina, who procured his banishment to the island of Corsica. His recall did not come until A.D. 49, when Claudius' ambitious fourth wife, Agrippina, arranged for him to be tutor to her son, Nero, who became emperor in A.D. 54.

With Seneca's recall in A.D. 49 began the period of his greatest political influence, an ascendancy which lasted until at least A.D. 59, and, in a more limited way, until A.D. 62. Thereafter, Nero appears to have become increasingly suspicious of him. Distrust came to a head with the disclosure of the plot against Nero (A.D. 65), in which Seneca's nephew Lucan apparently played a major role. With the detection of the plot came the downfall not only of Lucan and Seneca, but of most of Seneca's circle of family and friends.

Seneca's Works

Most surviving Roman writers can be handily categorized either as poets or as authors of prose works. Seneca is unusual in that both poetic and prose works attributed to him have survived from antiquity. The poetic works that have come down to us under his name are one historical drama, nine tragedies, which we will discuss shortly, and some epigrams in the *Latin Anthology*. In prose he wrote twelve books of *Dialogues*, the lengthy essays *On Clemency* and *On Benefits*, 124 letters to his friend Lucilius, seven books of *Natural Questions*, and a satire on the death of Claudius, the *Apocolocyntosis*—"*Pumpkinification.*" In these works, Seneca portrays himself as a member of the Stoic school of philosophy, though he frequently cites with admiration—and uses—ideas from rival intellectual groups, notably the Epicureans. Seneca's openness to ideas from different philosophical schools makes an interesting contrast with the hostility other philosophical writers of the first and second centuries A.D. show towards their intellectual opponents. To give two illustrative examples: The closest surviving ancient parallels to Seneca's satirical *Apocolocyntosis* are probably the *Dialogues of the Gods*, written by the Greek Epicurean Lucian a century or so later. Lucian is not nearly so kind to the Stoics, however, as Seneca is to the Epicureans. He mocks them mercilessly. Similarly, the closest parallel to Seneca's famous treatise *On Anger*, included among the *Dialogues*, is Plutarch's *On Anger*. Plutarch, however, had no patience with Stoicism and wrote two stinging essays, along with extensive negative comments elsewhere, attacking what he considered the absurdities of Stoic philosophy: *On Stoic Self-Contradictions* and *Against the Stoics on Common Conceptions*.

I mention these points because scholars sometimes interpret Seneca's poetry not just in terms of the Stoic elements in his philosophical prose, but as if he were an embodiment of the fundamentalist puritanism we find in Lucian's Stoic caricatures. They thus discover in his tragedies a kind of drama of Stoic dogmatism which accords ill with Seneca's—and Stoic—eclecticism, and with the Stoics' preoccupation with paradox. Yet even if we choose to believe Seneca was a Stoic zealot of the sort Lucian mocks, we do not have to see him as a soul that is self-confident and at spiritual peace. The religious and philosophical agonies of Milton or, no less poignantly, Donne, should warn us of the terrible "laceration of mind," as Samuel Johnson calls it, with which deep-seated religious feelings and conversions are associated. The same John Donne can, in other moods and times, produce the erotic flippancy of *The Flea* and the melancholy religious brilliance of *A Hymne to God the Father*. Similarly, Seneca will sometimes assure us of the invincibility of good, at other times confront us with the apparently inevitable triumph of evil.

The believer may struggle for footing over an abyss of atheism that the conventionally pious or the mere agnostic cannot begin to comprehend. Indeed, the eclecticism of Seneca's prose works might even emanate from the tolerance born in one who has experienced the agony of the abyss. Plato's Socrates in *Republic* 8–10 recognizes and fears the force of evil within the soul, the beast that awakens when the rational part of the mind is asleep. This irrational element, the mythical beast, must, he felt, be suppressed in each of us just as poetry must be suppressed within the state, at least in part because it gives form to the nightmarish and irrational. But to argue for the suppression of a passion or of an artistic form is to acknowledge one's fear of its power.

Seneca, unlike Plato, gives us two separate visions: the rational, philosophical obverse of his paradoxical coin and the poetical reverse. In fact, it is hard to be sure which side is the front and which the back of the Senecan coin. To get the complete picture, we must of course consider both. Nonetheless, it is entirely possible to contemplate each face separately. Students of Senecan philosophy have had no qualms about omitting discussion of the tragedies. Poets, therefore, have a precedent for the same sort of omission, but in reverse. We will, I would argue, gain a better picture of Seneca's poetry— and perhaps of his prose too—if we consider his tragedies, at least at first, *apart from* his prose works. For to do so will help us counteract a widely held but usually false assumption that poetry begins its existence as prose, and is, essentially, no more than a kind of ornate prose.

The manuscript tradition of Seneca's tragedies aids our task. For the plays, in fact, survived from antiquity separately from the prose works. Centuries ago it was thought that the poetry and prose were the works of two distinct persons: a tragic Seneca and a philosophical Seneca. So the question naturally arises: How do we know that the tragedies and the prose works were written by the same hand? Quintilian's quotation of *Medea* 354 in *Instructing the Orator* 9.2.8 is the only evidence that someone named Seneca actually wrote any of the plays that have come down to us under this name. Quintilian's phrase, "like Medea in Seneca," shows that (a) Seneca wrote it. But Quintilian may mean the Elder Seneca, as he clearly does later in the same chapter (9.2.42).

Settling the Senecan authorship of *Medea* still leaves unresolved the question as to whether the other nine plays included in the Senecan corpus are also by a Seneca. There is general consensus that one, *Octavia*, is not his work, and serious doubts have been raised about another, *Hercules on Oeta*. Most scholars accept the authenticity of the remaining seven—*Hercules in His Madness*, *Trojan Women*, *Phoenician Women*, *Phaedra*, *Oedipus*, *Agamemnon*, and *Thyestes*—even though, as we have seen, none of them is attested as Senecan by an ancient writer. I accept the judgment of scholars on the matter of the plays' authenticity, though I have a nagging suspicion that the *Elder* Seneca wrote *Phaedra* and, possibly, other plays.

Dating the Plays

Seneca is one of only a handful of Romans of senatorial rank before the fourth century A.D. who have survived to us as poets in their own right. Curiously, his most notable fellow aristocratic poets are his near contemporaries: his short-lived nephew Lucan (A.D. 39–65), author of the *Pharsalia*, and Silius Italicus (A.D. 25–101), author of the *Punica*. Like Lucan, and unlike Silius, Seneca appears to have written poetry while he was politically active. Yet Seneca differs sharply from Lucan as well as from Silius in several major respects. To begin with, they wrote epic, the most "elevated" of Roman poetic forms, and their epics show the self-confident moral and historical judgment that characterizes Roman senatorial writing. Their style is evocative of the aristocratic historians Sallust and Tacitus. They write of Rome itself, they lament the passage of a pluralistic, republican state. One is always aware of their Romanness and of the age in which they are writing.

Seneca, in contrast, not only chose tragedy, a literary form that had, by his time, ceased to be a major vehicle of poetic or political statement, but seems calculatedly to have avoided specific references both to his own day and to things Roman. Among the ten plays attributed to him, only *Octavia* deals with a contemporary subject. And few scholars now claim that this play was actually written by Seneca. In fact, Seneca is a character in it.

With the exception, then, of the *Octavia*, the plays attributed to Seneca present so few overt and recognizably Roman elements that

13

we are startled when we come upon them. This lack of contemporary reference makes dating the plays virtually impossible. The prose works, in contrast, are of much more certain date, ranging from his *Consolation to Marcia* (included among the *Dialogues*) in A.D. 41 to his *Natural Questions* and *Letters to Lucilius*, both published between A.D. 63 and 65.

Although the traditional, mythical topics Seneca selects for his plays are as obviously appropriate to the world of the early emperors at Rome as the mythical epics written by Statius and Valerius Flaccus in the decades just after Seneca's death, Seneca affords us no clues, as Statius does, about when his work was written and about what contemporary experience it refracts. We can hardly move beyond generalization. True, Seneca's plays, with the possible exception of *Phaedra*, mirror a top-heavy Roman world of absolute power as surely as Athenian tragedy mirrors the often chaotic Greek democracy and intellectual pluralism of Athens in the fifth century B.C. But, as Seneca lived his whole life under the imperial autocracy, we have not said much when we have said that.

Since dating the plays on external evidence and internal contemporary commentary is impossible, the best we can do is establish some probable sequence of their composition on the basis of internal stylistic considerations, as John Fitch has done.[3] Fitch accepts the general dating of *Hercules in His Madness* to before 54 B.C. This was the year of Claudius' death and Nero's accession to the throne. And one of Seneca's own works, the *Apocolocyntosis*, "*Pumpkinification*," parodies a lament from *Hercules in His Madness*. Fitch's study suggests that *Trojan Women* and *Medea* belong to approximately the same time period and that *Phaedra*, *Oedipus*, and *Agamemnon* are earlier. How much earlier, however, we cannot say. The fragmentary *Phoenician Women* and *Thyestes* were, according to Fitch's analysis written later, during the last decade of Seneca's life.

If Fitch is right—and there is no certain means of telling whether he is or not—Seneca's plays were written at various points throughout his life, but most *before* Nero's reign.

---

[3] "Sense-Pauses and Relative Dating in Seneca, Sophocles, and Shakespeare," *American Journal of Philology* 102 (1981): 289–307.

Critics and Admirers

Seneca was one of the most influential political, intellectual, and literary figures whose works survive to us from antiquity. He shaped the development of the tragic drama in Renaissance Europe, he inspired and influenced literary and intellectual figures as different as Montaigne and Calvin. In short, his appeal to creative writers has been immense. Yet the reader of modern articles and books about Seneca is more likely to encounter unfavorable than favorable critical evaluations of his work.

Hostility to Seneca is hardly new. From his own day on, Seneca's work and character have endured severe attacks from what we might loosely term the academic establishment. Writing less than a generation after Seneca's death, the rhetorician Quintilian takes him to task for a variety of errors in judgment and in style: the researchers he employed made mistakes; Seneca himself used "unnatural" expressions and strove to achieve a kind of terse "quotability." Seneca was, it seemed, a dangerous and potentially corrupting influence on a schoolboy's style of writing. Quintilian's reaction to Seneca was so strongly negative that some of his contemporaries thought it arose from personal loathing—an allegation Quintilian feels constrained to deny in his *Instructing the Orator*. The Roman historian Tacitus, writing shortly after Quintilian, passes similarly scathing judgment on Seneca's character: he was a hypocritically pious moralist with bloodied hands who lacked the courage of his convictions.

The negative scholarly view of Seneca did not gain the upper hand until the last two centuries, however. For the preceding millennium and a half, Seneca retained his following outside the classroom. Indeed, it was his enormous popularity as a literary figure in Quintilian's day which prompted the scholar to treat him at length, and in a special category apart from other writers, as a subversive literary model. After the early nineteenth century, however, Seneca lost his wide and admiring audience. Quintilian's anxieties about Seneca's corrupting influence were echoed by many Latin teachers who chose to instruct their students in the prose style of Caesar and Cicero and in the verse of Horace and Vergil. These teachers, too, found Seneca a corrupting influence who did not fit, and therefore undermined, firmly held notions of what a classical author should be both stylistically and morally. Seneca, like Apuleius and Statius, had to be rejected, however important he may have been in shaping Western literature, because he was "late," decadent, and "not classical." He did not represent the kind of Latinity, the period of Roman history, or the perspective on the Roman world that academics wanted to teach. And Seneca's critics found in Quintilian and Tacitus stylistic and moral justification for rejecting him.

Nineteenth- and twentieth-century scholarly antagonism to Seneca proved more damaging than Quintilian's attacks precisely because Seneca had lost his wider audience outside academia. It is important to understand, however, that his diminished popularity was not testimony to a change in literary tastes, as is sometimes suggested, but to the fact that Latin literature as a whole had become increasingly the exclusive and dwindling domain of academics who often seemed curiously determined to show how distasteful most of it was while lamenting that people were neglecting it. No field of literary study rivals that of Latin poetry in so systematically belittling the quality of its works and authors. And no field of literary study more thoroughly quarantines itself from contemporary critical thought. As a result, in many colleges Seneca is outside the still decreasing canon of academically "approved" writers, as are the overwhelming majority of ancient writers whose works are extant but unread even in excerpts.

Latinists often forget how many of the "faults" for which they denounce Seneca and other Roman writers are, in fact, the usual goals towards which poets and essayists strive: to make the language their own rather than to follow scholastically prescribed usage; to avail themselves of all the resonances of meaning their language can bear; to achieve the memorable, the quotable. The criticisms directed against Seneca by Quintilian and his successors could even more justifiably be leveled against Shakespeare: he, too, made mistakes in research, used "unnatural" expressions, and strove to achieve terse "quotability."

But recently the picture has been changing. Major critical editions of Senecan tragedy by Tarrant (*Agamemnon*, *Thyestes*), Fantham (*Tro-*

jan Women), Fitch's *Hercules,* and Costa's smaller *Medea* have begun
to focus classicists' attention on Senecan drama. And although—or
rather because—Seneca has ceased to be canonical reading, interest
in his works, especially in his tragedies, has gradually reawakened
among poets, historians of the theater, and Shakespearean critics.
The ascendancy of what scholars and directors alike have taken to be
the Greek model of tragedy became so marked and ubiquitous by
the middle of the twentieth century that the Greek muse was no
longer exotic. Sophocles seemed familiar. The Roman Seneca now
became the remote, primitive, and mysterious writer. Roman tragedy had been absent from the canonical reading of our culture long
enough for its rediscovery to be exciting and artistically stimulating.
It was "other," it was malleable, it was the stuff of experiment and
innovation in the theater. And that, Ted Hughes observed, is why
Peter Brook wanted to produce Seneca's, not Sophocles', *Oedipus* in
London at the Old Vic in 1968.

The differences between Senecan and Athenian tragedy are often—
as they were to the producers of Ted Hughes' adaptation of Seneca's
Oedipus—precisely the strength and theatrical allure of the Latin dra-
mas. As Hughes wrote in his introduction to *Oedipus,* "the Greek
world saturates Sophocles too thoroughly: the evolution of his play
seems complete, fully explored and in spite of its blood-roots, fully
civilized. The figures in Seneca's *Oedipus* are Greek only by conven-
tion: by nature they are more primitive than aboriginals . . . . Seneca
hardly notices the intricate moral possibilities of his subject."[4]

I do not much agree with Hughes' assessment of Senecan as opposed
to Sophoclean drama, since I believe that Sophocles, no less than
Seneca, has been distorted by the puzzling modern desire to treat
tragedies as moral and religious sermons. But this disagreement is
beside the point. Hughes' essential point is, I think, correct: Senecan
tragedy is vastly and intriguingly different from Greek tragedy. To
contend that Seneca is doing no more than rendering some extant or
nonextant Greek original is to do him the injustice that scholars have
finally, I hope, stopped doing Plautus. The contrast, then, between
Hughes' notion of Senecan tragedy and the conventional scholarly

---

[4] *Seneca's "Oedipus,"* adapted by Ted Hughes (London, 1969), p. 8.

view of Seneca could hardly be more total. Hughes is delighted that Seneca is un-Greek; classicists are upset that Seneca is not Greek enough.

Seneca's characters are more introspective and self-analyzing than even a Sophoclean Ajax. Their most critical battles, like the critical battles of many a Shakespearean character, are often those that they fight with themselves. Senecan drama constantly takes us beyond a character's words into his or her very thoughts, keeping us aware of the tension between what someone says and does and what that same person perceives as the reason for what is said and done. We see a character's hopes, illusions, and delusions played out before us.

Seneca and the Theater

Increased theatrical interest in Senecan tragedy contrasts with scholastic insistence that Senecan tragedy was never actually staged at Rome. We will never know if and how Senecan tragedy was staged. It is probably correct that Seneca's *Oedipus* was not produced before the massed citizen body of Rome as Sophocles' *Oedipus* was produced before the citizen body of Athens. But this does not mean it was not designed for performance and actually performed in small gatherings, as we shall see. Much modern drama is not aimed at, or performed before, a broad national audience either. Despite the accessibility of mass audiences through television and cinema, the contemporary writer often chooses to address a literary elite in a small theater.

Although Seneca clearly writes for an elite too, his plays deal with and direct themselves towards the powerful, as most modern theater in the English language does not. Senecan tragedy, like Greek, is about power and about those who exercise it, and it addresses the issues of power through the language of myth. It does not name contemporary names; it speaks through traditional characters drawn ultimately from an ancient poetic tradition whose roots extend back into the second millennium B.C. and beyond. Yet the fact that Senecan tragedy deals with and directs itself to the powerful is the reason it can be seen not only to resemble classical Greek tragedy but, paradoxically, to differ from Greek tragedy when one inspects it more closely.

18

During the Athenian democracy, poetic expression was dominantly theatrical. The Athenian audience that listened in the theater voted in the assembly; poets, like the popular leaders, sought to reach it and persuade it. Roman poets of the early empire, and those of pre- and post- democratic Greece, directed their work to the literate ruling classes, and shied away from "popular" drama. First, the populace had no political power in imperial Rome. It could not even vote to elect magistrates. That is why I find the Chorus' remarks in *Phaedra* 982–984 perplexing. Its words seem to suggest that the populace exercises a political role which it did not in Seneca's day:

> fraud rules as despot　in the halls of power,
> the people find joy　in giving high office [*fasces*]
> to a vile man. They　adore those they hate most.

Second, under the Roman emperors it was difficult and dangerous, as well as, apparently, futile, to communicate with the popular audience. If a popular audience detected a covert insult or jest at the emperor's expense, it might be unsophisticated enough to roar its recognition, approving or disapproving, aloud—to the great peril of the writer. Smaller, more refined audiences, meeting in times of tyranny and in gatherings where names are known, react more cautiously. Experience teaches them that to acknowledge the insult or the jest, or even to be present when it is made, imperils the listener as well as the author. That is why, in a notorious incident mentioned by the biographer Suetonius in his life of Seneca's nephew Lucan, the people in a public restroom fled when Lucan, while breaking wind noisily, quoted a half-line written by the emperor Nero.

Besides, the literary theater never enjoyed in Rome the official state support it had in Athens. There were no permanent theaters until Pompey built one in 55 B.C. And that great general built it to give himself, not dramatists, a stage. Actors, as well as some playwrights, were often slaves or former slaves, not members of a fashionable profession. Further, dramatists had to compete for the public's attention with spectacles of increasing scale and extravagance that were underwritten by the wealthy and sanctioned by ritual practice. The Latin word *munus*, suggesting a public offering or service, came to be shorthand for a gladiatorial "offering." Such ritual and circus-like

19

entertainments were features of Roman life from the middle of the third century B.C. on. The ruling classes stressed the spectacular and underplayed the verbal and intellectual dimensions so fundamental to Greek drama. Terence, the comic playwright, in the prologue to *The Mother- in-Law*, says it was impossible to hold one's own against the competition of a tightrope walker. Holding one's own against a gladiatorial "offering" would have been no easier.

The poet Horace, writing in Rome a generation or two before Seneca, tells Octavian, the imperial Augustus, that Democritus—"the laughing philosopher," as he was called—would guffaw at the notion that a dramatist could win the attention of his restive audience: "he would think the writers were creating their play for an ass—and a deaf one. What voices have had power enough to overwhelm the noise which echoes round our theaters?" (Horace *Epistles* 2.1.199–201). Pleasure, Horace adds, has "shifted from the ear to eyes that are not good at seeing" (*Epistles* 2.1.187–188), even among the Equestrian order, the Roman upper middle class. And, he continues in the lines immediately following, not only games but triumphal processions celebrating military victories have intruded upon the dramatist's stage.

Horace' last comment has a special pungency in this epistle, addressed as it is to Octavian, who had been the victor in a savage civil war and was the conqueror and imperial ruler of Rome. If the biographer Suetonius is right in his claim that this poem is Horace's response to Octavian's complaint of exclusion from Horace's *sermones*, his "conversations"—the works we know as his *Satires* and *Epistles*—Horace is suggesting that the emperor, as principal giver of games and sole giver of triumphs, has usurped the dramatist's place in the theater. The theater is owned by the emperor and stages only his shows. Hence Horace's expressed desire to entrust himself to a *reader* rather than to a spectator (*Epistles* 2.1.214–218). The language and metaphor he uses are more appropriate to the arena and the hippodrome than to the muses and god of poetry. They suggest that Octavian thinks more in terms of a *munus*, "offering," than of poetry itself. He wants books that will fight for him like gladiators, that will serve his glory. The theater already exists for the emperor's glory; the threat lurks that all literature will come to serve the same purpose.

For Octavian now wishes to intrude himself into the poet's private "conversations."

Octavian was, in fact, more eager to censor published and *durable* poetry than the more fleeting criticism which might occur in a public performance. Ovid, who died in exile when Seneca was in his teens, chastises Octavian for being so concerned about morality in poetry but so unconcerned about the blatant immorality of what is represented in the theater and at the emperor's own games, before his very eyes (*Tristia* 2.497–546). In *Tristia* 5.7.25–30, Ovid comments on the irony of his own situation in this regard: some of his poetry has been adapted for and performed in the theater, although he himself claims: "I have—and you know this yourself—written nothing for the theater." Incidentally, if we take Ovid at his work here, the two lines said to have survived from his play *Medea* would seem either not to be genuinely his or to be adapted from his treatments of Medea elsewhere in his poetry. He may, of course, have written the work for reading or performance elsewhere than in the public theater. Still, in his exile, he says, he takes some consolation in the thought that his poems, adapted for the theater, keep his memory and name alive in Rome.

The theater, then, was seen by both poet and political leader in the generations preceding Seneca not only as a noisy place, unconducive to poetry, but as a vehicle of corruption and political propaganda. Succeeding Roman emperors, particularly Nero and Domitian, were also well aware of the theater's power. Domitian banned actors from the public stage. Nero adopted a much different approach. Part of his own immense popularity—and much of the contempt that men of letters felt for him—stemmed from his appearances as a performer in the theater and the hippodrome.

Despite their reluctance to write for the popular stage, Roman writers were aware—in Ovid's case poignantly aware—that performances in the theater have a power over the popular imagination that "pure" poetry lacks, and they regularly presented human activity in terms of the theater or amphitheater. In his *Aeneid*, Vergil describes the landscape of North Africa as a *scaena*, a stage set, and compares the nightmarish visions of Queen Dido to the horror experienced on stage by Pentheus or Orestes. When Aeneas visits the new Troy built by Andromache, he walks in on a tragic tableau: a mock Troy frozen in time, as if in a painting or stage set, with Andromache lamenting, as ever, over an empty grave honoring her dead husband, Hector. The characters of Latin poetry also see themselves theatrically or amphitheatrically. In Lucan's *Pharsalia*, Pompey, builder of Rome's first permanent theater, dreams of his past triumphs in theatrical imagery. As he dies, he behaves like an actor who must win approval for his final scene. Lucan, in fact, gives an important role in the *Pharsalia* to the man who invented the amphitheater: Scribonius Curio. And this Curio, we are told by the historian and naturalist Pliny, a contemporary of Seneca's, was the same man who maneuvered the opposing political factions of the Roman state into civil war, much as he turned his two back-to-back theaters into one amphitheater to stage a grand gladiatorial contest.

Seneca presents life in terms of the arena both in his tragedies and in his philosophical works. In his essay *On Providence* he dismisses ordinary gladiatorial shows as "the childish delights of human vanity" and asks us to contemplate instead the greatest contest of them all: "a matched pair worthy of god's eyes—a brave man pitted against an evil destiny, with the brave man as challenger." In his tragedies, particularly *Trojan Women*, many motifs suggest a theater far different from that of Aeschylus or Euripides. The site of Polyxena's sacrifice on Achilles' tomb, for example, is described as if it were part of a *munus*, an offering, in the amphitheater (*Trojan Women* 1123–1126):

> on the other side,
> it [the tomb] is encompassed by a plain, rising
> gently at the edges to create
> a valley in between—the shape suggests
> a theater, in fact.

Astyanax' death has much the same "theatrical" quality. The dramatist asks his audience and readers to envisage the scene from Greek myth in terms of the familiar horror of ritual death in the Roman theater. And he asks them to censure those who hated what they saw but watched anyway. Roman readers could hardly fail to see themselves reflected in the Senecan mirror, much as they would see themselves in the equally stinging comment in the passage from *Phaedra*, cited earlier, that they worship those holders of the *fasces* (the Roman symbols of public office) whom they hate. Yet Seneca is aware that he, like his morally critical messenger, is himself as guilty of hypocrisy as those he criticizes.

At least one of Seneca's tragic characters, the messenger whom I would identify with Talthybius in *Trojan Women*, recognizes how sacrificial and gladiatorial death affects the spectator: desire to watch vying with hatred of what one watches. Seneca understands that part of his audience will see the victims as heroic and that such heroism is beyond words. The doomed Polyxena in *Trojan Women* does not speak; Astyanax says only "Pity me, mother." In the verbal environment of tragedy, the sacrificial heroes themselves do not speak. They, like the Chorus envisaging cosmic catastrophe in the *Thyestes*, invite the listener or reader to imagine, not to hear. Seneca, like other great writers of Roman imperial times, often creates images for the mind's eye rather than for strictly visual perception.

The model that Seneca's Roman reader or listener used as his imagination wandered could be drawn from memories of the countless silent "performers" who died each year at Roman games. This same amphitheatrical notion of heroic death helped the growth of Christianity. The martyrs who died in the arena recalled the secularized contests to their ritual origins. And the horror of their suffering fixed another myth in men's minds.

To interest a popular Roman audience in a stage "death" when the games afforded ample opportunity to see real death must have been difficult. The dramatist could not compete, and probably would not have wanted to compete, with the grim spectacles Martial, a poet of the generation after Seneca, describes in his *Book of Spectacles*. The Roman amphitheater imparted to even the grossest and most grisly myths a certain air of reality. The emperor Titus staged not only Hercules' labors at the games in real-life performances but the consummation of the Cretan queen Pasiphae's obsessive passion for a bull. Pasiphae was the wife of Minos, king of Crete, and she was helped in her desire to mate with the bull by the Athenian artist Daedalus, who designed a cowsuit for her to wear so that the bull would mistake her for a heifer. Her child by this union was, of course, the famous Minotaur:

Believe it now! Pasiphae did make it with the Cretan bull;
  We've seen it happen; the old story now has credibility.
Yet ancient folklore should not take the credit for itself:
  Caesar, your circus actors make *all* folksongs live for you.

In the following poems Martial reiterates his point about the "realization" of myth on stage. Poem 7 is the culmination of the series.:

Just as Prometheus, bound tight on a Russian crag
Fed with his ever-healing and regrowing heart
The bird that never tires of eating
                    So,
                        cast as Laureolus,
The bandit-king, nailed to a cross (no stage-prop this)
The unknown actor showed his raw guts to a Highland bear.
His shredded limbs clung onto life although
Their bits and pieces gushed with blood:
No trace of body—but the body lived.
Finally he got the punishment he deserved . . . [5]
  Maybe he'd slit his master's throat, the thug;
  Maybe he'd robbed a temple treasury of gold, mad fool;
  Maybe he'd tried to burn our city, Rome.
The criminal responsible surpassed all ancient folklore's crimes.
Through him what had been merely myth became
  Real punishment.

The condemned criminal—whose crime, we note, no one seems to know for sure—is condemned to act out the role of Laureolus, the bandit-king, crucified in the arena.

The cruelty Martial describes was not Titus' invention. Titus was merely continuing a tradition begun by the emperor Caligula. Suetonius, the biographer of the earliest emperors, describes the bloody competition for the role of Laureolus in Caligula's day in his *Life of Caligula*. But what Martial sets first in our minds is the myth of Prometheus: the benefactor of mankind, enduring the daily attacks of the bird that fed on his liver and knowing the secret that would

---

[5] Part of the line is lost in our texts.

24

bring about the downfall of his tormentor, the god Jupiter. The comparison with the man playing Laureolus, then, horrifies with its appropriate inappropriateness. Myth tells us how Prometheus offended Jupiter, but it also reassures us of his ultimate release by Hercules. Martial's nameless criminal, however, guilty of crimes unknown, will have no Hercules to free him, and a wild bear, not a surgically precise bird's beak, will torment him. The poor substitute Laureolus, whatever he did, earns the status of Prometheus, which, in this incident, gives him a greater claim to divinity than any of the emperors who often pretended that they were themselves gods: Jupiter incarnate. Martial's Laureolus walks the same "stage" as the suffering Christ.

Martial, the poet-artist, does not specifically thank his emperor for this demonstration of myth's viability (as he thanks him in each of the preceding poems), surely because the poem is a terrible indictment of what his eyes have seen and thus of whoever it was that organized the grim spectacle. Martial had some reason to be cautious. For, as poem 8 makes clear, the artist himself may endure a similarly mythlike fate:

> Artistic Daedalus:
>   When you were being wolfed and mangled by that bear
>   How you must have wished you now had your wings!

Daedalus, having helped Pasiphae mate with the bull, later designed the labyrinth to conceal her child. He also helped Theseus kill the beast and escape with Minos' daughter Ariadne. Understandably, he lost his royal master's favor. Minos imprisoned him in his own work of art. Daedalus escaped by inventing wings and flying out. Martial's latter-day Daedalus, however, out of favor with his Minos, has no wings to escape his enraged master and the carnivorous beast.

The Roman imperial poet's task was dauntingly Daedalus-like. Aware that he served an often cruel master, he had to communicate without ending up like Martial's Daedalus. The poet knew he could not compete for an audience of the moment with the spectacle, with the reality of Roman theatrical death. He could not even express his full disgust with that spectacle, his horror at it—much less attempt to aid its victims—without risking a terrible fate himself. In the first satire of Juvenal, a near contemporary of Martial, we are told of a critic whose charred corpse inscribes a black line in the sand of the theater after he has been used as a human torch to light the arena. The poet risks being transformed from a writer into a pen with which others write. Hence, perhaps, his flight from and fascination with the theater, his preference for epic and for myth. As Martial shows, only myth could express the extent of the horror of what was happening precisely *because* even myth paled in comparison with the staged reality. Life, as presented in the arena, had become an imitation of art. Ovid, in his *Metamorphoses*, suggests it always had been.

Staging the Plays

Senecan tragedy demands performance, not just recitation by two or three readers. The rapid interchanges between, say, Medea (or Phaedra) and her nurse need actors, not just voices. The commonly held view that the plays were recited by a single voice assumes that the Latin terms *recitare* and *recitatio* carry the same sense as the English "recite" and "recitation." There is no reason, however, to suppose that they preclude the notion of performance by multiple actors, much as *recitare* does in Italian theatrical parlance. *Recitare un dramma* means "to perform a play," not "to recite a play." What is sometimes called the "Recitation theory" of Senecan tragedy owes much both to this restrictive Anglo-German-French sense of what *recitatio* must have been and to the low opinion scholars hold of Senecan tragedy as theater. Many Latinists, I am sure, would agree with Elaine Fantham's observation that Seneca's tragedies "are not well-crafted stage-plays."[6] I disagree. Having staged three of the plays, and served as an adviser in the production of a fourth, I have been surprised at how effective they are as theater. Scholars exaggerate the difficulties of staging them and undervalue their theatrical innovations, perhaps to justify their view of the tragedies as one-man recitations.

None of the complete plays attributed to Seneca presents major staging problems to a director, much less difficulties comparable to

[6] *Seneca's "Troades": A Literary Introduction with Text, Translation, and Commentary* (Princeton, 1982), p. 49. See now Dana Sutton's excellent *Seneca on the Stage*, Mnemosyne Supplement 96 (Leiden, 1986).

those found in such Greek tragedies as Sophocles' *Ajax* or Aeschylus' *Eumenides* (which *were* publicly performed). Once we accept Senecan tragedy as designed for performance, we may appreciate better some of the remarkable effects, actual and potential, in the staging of *Phaedra*, *Medea*, and *Trojan Women*. In *Trojan Women*, for instance, Seneca brings Pyrrhus onstage to take Polyxena away to be sacrificed. Pyrrhus and Polyxena move but do not speak. Yet they are spoken to by Hecuba and Andromache. In forceful contrast, Hecuba and Andromache, though they speak, are not involved in the *action* of the scene.

Yet if, as I have suggested, the plays were designed for performance but not performed in public theaters, were they only plays in search of a stage, or were they performed but in a less public manner? The germ of an answer is found in Suetonius' *Domitian* 7. Domitian, we are told, "forbade actors to use the [outdoor, public] stage, but conceded to them the right to practice their art indoors." Domitian's action, of course, was taken some thirty years after Seneca's death. But the practice of "in-house" performances may well have been going on for some time before Domitian's decree. And this, I believe, is how Senecan tragedy was performed: in the more than ample homes of well-to-do Romans. I emphasize that my resolution of the problem is no more than a matter of personal opinion—as are other theories about the performance or nonperformance of the plays. I also warn the reader that stage directions given in the translations are only my suggestions. Recall, however, that stage directions found in translations of Greek tragedy are also the work of a translator—though he or she does not always acknowledge this to be the case.

Ultimately the question as to how Senecan tragedy was presented matters more to a historian of the theater than to a director. The real question for the director is whether he would find one of these plays stageworthy if he had a usable script in hand. And here is the major problem: there are few English versions of Senecan tragedy and even fewer which suggest that the plays are stageworthy. My aim has been to produce stageable versions of the plays without resorting to adaptation rather than translation and without sacrificing the poetry in an effort to achieve colloquial realism. For Senecan tragedy, like Shakespearean or Greek tragedy, is a poetic form, not just a dramatic one.

About the Translations

Translating Seneca is hampered not only by critical prejudice against the plays but by an increasing tendency to disparage Latin literature as a whole. Latin has been for centuries the language of learning and of pretentiousness. And, unlike Greek, its latter-day scholastic rival, it has a rather English appearance, since so many English words are derived either directly or indirectly from Latin. It is remote enough to appear abstract and pedantic but too familiar to seem exotic. If Erich Auerbach had called his book *Imitatio* rather than *Mimesis*, it would probably have had less appeal. To caricature the popular stereotypes: the Greeks, who were imaginative, practiced mimesis; the Romans, good at building arches but less adept at poetry and philosophy, practiced imitation. These stereotypes are well established in English-speaking societies. And Latinists themselves are largely responsible for them.

Although many English words look as if they should be equivalents for their Latin ancestors, they often differ greatly in meaning or "feel." We would rarely assume that the character of a remote ancestor can correctly be assessed by analyzing the character of a modern descendant of the same name. Yet we are sometimes less than cautious in making similar assumptions about English words of Latin ancestry. "Accept," for example, derives from the Latin *accipere*, which means something like "to take to oneself." The English "accept" lacks the aggressive sense of *accipere*. It comes from a passive form of the Latin verb and retains a sense of passivity, as do a great many words used in Latinate English. The lethargy of the descendants belies their ancestral vigor. Yet popular dictionaries and translations still use the descendants to represent their forefathers, largely because scholars cannot agree on alternatives. "Virtue," derived from *virtus*, is a good instance, especially because here we are concerned with a Roman writer who had much to say about *virtus*. Ancient Roman *virtus*, not out of place on the battlefield, evolved into the now obsolete "virtue" as philosophers, moralists, and monks adapted it for use in a sexual context.[7] At the beginning of the twentieth century Francis Cornford,

---

[7] "Virtue," in all likelihood, died when its own adjective, "virtuous," was found unacceptable by movie censors in Hollywood in the 1930s. Presumably virtue's foes

in the introduction to his translation of Plato's *Republic*, satirized the use of "virtue" as a translation for the Greek *arete*: "One who opened Jowett's version at random and lighted on the statement . . . that the best guardian for a man's 'virtue' is 'philosophy tempered with music,' might run away with the idea that, in order to avoid irregular relations with women, he had better play the violin in the intervals of studying metaphysics."[8] Subsequent Greek scholars have dealt with the problem not by seeking another equivalent but by adopting *arete* into their usage as a translation for itself. Latinists, in contrast, generally retain "virtue" for *virtus*. Those embarrassed by "virtue" yet fearful of scholarly scorn for using an English term which misses many nuances of *virtus* cautiously imitate the Hellenist and use *virtus* as a translation for itself. Such subterfuge is available to the scholarly commentator but not to the translator. And I have tried to avoid it. Obviously my choice, "manliness," will not please everyone. But it does try to bring out the force of *vir*, "man," in *virtus* even though it cannot catch the paradoxically feminine gender of the Latin original.

The translator must take into account other differences between Latin and English. Latin is compact and polysyllabic. English is more monosyllabic and far more compact. There are inevitably more words in an English sentence than in its Latin original, but not necessarily more *syllables*. I have tried to keep the number of syllables in my English approximately equal to the number of syllables in Seneca's Latin. Since the English iambic pentameter used here in place of the Latin trimeter is syllabically shorter, however, there are more lines in my English then in the Latin. For the reader's convenience, I mark the line numbers of the Latin original in the margins.

To convey the force and style of Senecan tragedy, something must be done with his ubiquitous wordplay. It is insufficient, when translating poetry, to select the word in language *A* which most closely approximates what scholars take to be the meaning of a given word

---

realized that if someone were described as "not virtuous," audiences would naturally assume that he or she was sexually active. Mention of sexual activity was taboo in English and American films of the period. The RKO studio therefore instructed its writers to avoid words which suggested physical sexuality, however obliquely. "Virtuous" was one of the words proscribed (as was "nursery"). See K. MacGowan, *Behind the Screen* (New York, 1965), p. 358.

[8] *The "Republic" of Plato*, trans. F. M. Cornford (Oxford, 1941), p. vi.

in language *B*. Poetic word selection is rarely governed exclusively, or even largely, by considerations of what teachers call "literal" meaning. Seneca, like many poets, ancient and modern, creates a richly allusive text where the "literal" meaning of a word often explodes into wordplay of multiple resonances suggested by the context in which it is set. I render the wordplays I have detected (puns, anagrams, and so forth) by equivalent plays in English.

My translations aim at a formal but not stuffy American literary and poetic idiom, interspersed, where appropriate, with a more colloquial style to underscore changes of mood and tone in the original. A few residual Anglicisms from my British childhood may have crept in too. At the same time, I have avoided such Americanisms as might appear stridently alien in other English-speaking countries. My usage may therefore seem synthetic and artificially neutral. I would defend my choices in these matters on the grounds that Senecan tragedy is itself formal in style and diction, and in verse. The tragedies are poetry and cannot be transposed satisfactorily into modern, colloquial prose drama without radical departures from the structure of the original.

I found that each Senecan play had a very individual "feel." The characters are quite distinct from one another even when they have similar roles. Thus the nurse in the *Phaedra* and the nurse in the *Medea* are as distinctive as the protagonists they serve. Indeed, no preconception about Senecan drama strikes me as more fundamentally incorrect than the notion that each play is essentially a variant of one plot, rehashed with characters of a dull sameness. As I translated, what surprised me most was the ironic wit of such characters as Pyrrhus and the humorous yet horrifying pomposity of Agamemnon in the *Trojan Women*. It had not occurred to me before that Seneca, like Euripides, might be capable of enhancing our sense of horror by evoking laughter.

My approach to each play is different, partly by design, partly by accident. The elaborate choral metrics of the *Phaedra* seemed to need a more elaborate English response than the delectable but less complex metrics of the *Trojan Women*. So I chose to approximate the Latin meters more closely in the *Phaedra* than in the *Trojan Women*. On the other hand, I prepared these translations over a period of some fifteen years, finishing the *Trojan Women* first and the *Phaedra* last. During that period my approach to Latin poetry and translation has changed considerably. But I have tried not to edit out my earlier perceptions of the *Trojan Women*, my personal favorite among the tragedies. I believe it to be the finest piece of theater Seneca produced, comparable with the best of Greek drama.

Questions the Plays May Prompt

Seneca clearly assumed that his audience or readers were intimately familiar with Greco-Roman myth. To help the reader less familiar with these tales, I have prepared brief introductions to the myths underlying each play and appended a glossary. Where the translation makes an important but indirect allusion to a character or place, I have noted at the foot of the page the glossary entry under which the information can be found. Sometimes, of course, ancient writers made statements or allusions which were probably as obscure to their contemporaries as they are to us, and were probably intended to puzzle or stimulate thought. These questions I have not attempted to answer in the text, but have left for the reader or performer to resolve.

A play, let us remind ourselves, is like a musical score in that it does not really live until it is performed. And then it has as many potentially different forms as it has directors, actors, and critics. So in the individual introductions to the plays I have sketched some questions the reader may want to ask about the characters and their roles. Characters in good drama, as in real life, are not simply linear, consistent beings (as scholars sometimes try to make them). They behave differently in different situations. They contradict themselves, they are often torn between conflicting impulses and obligations. Senecan drama is much more firmly rooted in the conflicts within the individual mind than are most Greek tragedies. Understanding the characters and the play involves a search for those areas or—to use a geological metaphor—those faults where different segments of a personality threaten each other and, in a larger sense, the stability of the world about them.

The Latin texts of the tragedies used are, in general, those of Elaine Fantham (*Seneca's "Troades": A Literary Introduction with Text, Trans-*

lation, and Commentary [Princeton, 1982]), C. D. N. Costa (Seneca, *Medea* [Oxford, 1973]), and P. Grimal (*L. Annaei Senecae Phaedra*, Erasme, Collection de textes latins commentés 14 [Paris, 1965]). I am grateful to Wolfgang Haase and the de Gruyter Press for giving me permission to reuse a few pages of my article "The Rider and the Horse: Politics and Power in Roman Poetry from Horace to Statius," *Aufstieg und Niedergang der römischen Welt* 32.1 (Berlin/New York, 1984), pp. 40–110. And I owe many debts to the friends and scholars who have given me advice and criticism: John Fitch, Eleanor Winsor Leach, Elaine Fantham, David Konstan, Joan Jeffri, David Keller, Rajani Sudan, and to my classics students and colleagues at Cornell, the University of Otago in New Zealand, and the University of Texas at Austin who helped me stage them. Sincere thanks also go to Martha Linke and Georgia Nugent, who saved me from many errors; my fellow editors of the Masters of Latin Literature, Diskin Clay, Douglass Parker, and Jon Stallworthy; above all, to my wife, Mary.

PHAEDRA

Introduction to *Phaedra*

The Senecan *Phaedra* is one of two surviving ancient tragedies on the subject of Phaedra's obsession with her stepson, Hippolytus. The other is Euripides' *Hippolytus*. The two plays, however, differ substantially in their treatment of both plot and character.

Play and Myth

Senecan characters are not just fictions of the poet's imagination. Nor are they simply traditional mythic figures in a conventional literary environment over whose shape and behavior the writer has little or no control. They are poetic fictions built upon myths whose general significance was widely known among Greeks and Romans, even those with a minimal education. The Cretan princess Phaedra, for example, is the daughter of Pasiphae, whose name, in Greek, means "the one who shines on everything." Not surprisingly, Pasiphae is a daughter of the Sun. Phaedra's father is Minos, the son of Jupiter, the Sky God. Jupiter, disguised as a white bull, abducted a Phoenician princess, Europa, and carried her across the Mediterranean Sea. Europa ultimately gave birth to children by Jupiter in his bovine form: Minos, Rhadamanthys, and Sarpedon. Ancient writers identify this Jupiter disguised as a bull with the constellation Taurus. And Phaedra,

For further reading see A. J. Boyle's brilliant essay "In Nature's Bonds: A Study of Seneca's *Phaedra*," in *Aufstieg und Niedergang der römischen Welt* 32.3 (1985), pp. 1284–1347; also C. P. Segal's *Language and Desire in Seneca's "Phaedra"* (Princeton, 1986) (not available to me when this introduction was prepared).

daughter of Minos and Pasiphae, carries on the astral symbolism in her name, which means "the beaming one."

Not only is Minos a son of the celestial Jupiter disguised as a bull; but his name suggests the ancient Egyptian word for bull. The bovine connection is most famous in the tradition associated with Minos' wife, Pasiphae, who fell in love with a white bull. The bull myth, we see, is reversed in this second generation. Now it is the female, not the male, who yearns for the sexual liaison; the bull is simply an animal, not a god disguised.[1] Because the white bull is uninterested in her, Pasiphae asks an Athenian artist, Daedalus, to design in wood the hollow form of a cow. Entering this structure, she attracts and mates with the bull. Their child is the Minotaur, half bull, half man. Minos now asks Daedalus to design a prison to contain the monster: the labyrinth at Cnossos in Crete, a maze from which there is no escape. And Minos uses the Minotaur and the labyrinth as a means of punishing the Athenians, who killed his son, Androgeos: he orders them to send an annual sacrifice of seven youths and seven maidens to die in the labyrinth.

The Senecan Phaedra is painfully aware that she is half sister to a monster. She also has a beautiful sister, Ariadne. Ariadne had been Theseus' lover before Theseus married Phaedra; later she was transformed into a star by Bacchus, the god of wine.

Even in this sketch we can see why our Phaedra is torn between her celestial and animal identities. Other superhuman and subhuman elements in the Phaedra myth are also alluded to in the play. Phaedra's father, Minos, is not only the child of the bull that swam across the sea; he is also famous for establishing Cretan control over the sea. Further, ancient authors often treat Minos as a kind of lord of—or at least judge among—the dead. Thus the tradition of Minos contains elements that make him a double for both Neptune, the sea god, and Dis (or Pluto), god of the dead. The bull and the labyrinth become complex symbols of the sea and of death as well as of the skies.

---

[1]Such mythic reversals are common, as we see in a variant myth associated with the constellation Taurus. Some ancient writers say the constellation is not a bull but a cow who was originally a water nymph named Io, loved by Jupiter and transformed by Juno, Jupiter's jealous wife, into bovine form. But the imagery remains astral: Io is often identified with Isis, a horned Egyptian goddess whom Greeks and Romans thought symbolic of the moon.

Indeed, Theseus, who kills the Minotaur in the labyrinth, arrives by sea, is a child of the sea, and is one of the few Greek heroes who descends into, and returns from, the world of the dead. Theseus arrives with—or as one of—the fourteen victims to be sacrificed to the Minotaur. The number, fourteen, also has astral associations. The seven stars of Hyades and the seven Pleiades are the most notable features of the constellation Taurus, and the Minotaur is sometimes called Asterion, "the Starry One."[2]

In some traditions Theseus is the son of Aegeus, king of Athens; in others he is the son of Neptune, god of the sea.[3] Theseus is raised by his mother, Aethra, "Clear Sky," at Troizen in the Peloponnesus, where he stays until he becomes a young man. He then sets out for Athens to seek Aegeus, who is now married to Medea—a grandchild of the Sun. Medea, his jealous stepmother, tries to murder Theseus (hatred of stepmothers, we will see, is an important motif in our play). But Theseus survives and establishes his heroism by killing a wild bull which terrorized the neighborhood of Marathon in Attica. His skill in disposing of bulls is well established before he meets the Minotaur.

When Theseus sets out for Crete, his ship is equipped with black sails, which he promises his father he will exchange for white if he kills the Minotaur and returns home. On his arrival in Crete, Ariadne, Phaedra's sister, falls in love with him and resolves to help him. Daedalus also assists, providing Ariadne with spool of thread which she gives to Theseus to help him find his way out of the labyrinth after he has killed the Minotaur. Escaping from Crete, he takes Ariadne with him. But, on his way back to Athens, he abandons her on an island (Naxos), where she is later rescued by Bacchus.

Theseus neglects to change his ship's sails before arriving off the coast of Attica. His father, Aegeus, presumes him dead and throws himself into the sea. Theseus becomes king of Athens in his place. But his rule is not secure until he fights off the challenge of the Amazons, a race of female warriors who hate men and serve Diana,

---

[2]Daedalus, the labyrinth's architect, later takes to the skies to escape from the House of the Bull: he designed wings and flew out with his son, Icarus, who was destroyed because he soared too close to the sun.

[3]Since the Aegean Sea is named for Aegeus, who is linked with the cult of the sea god Neptune, we should not differentiate the versions too precisely.

the goddess of hunting and chastity. These women attempt to set up a rival city next to Theseus'. Theseus defeats them and rapes their queen, Antiope (sometimes called Hippolyte). Antiope bears a son, Hippolytus, whose name was thought to mean "the man destroyed by horses"—a name that is an omen of his doom. Given the solar imagery associated with both Theseus' and Minos' families, the story of Hippolytus' death often evokes comparison with the tale of Phaethon, "the Fiery One," the child of the Sun who was unable to control the solar chariot. The Milky Way was, according to some ancient writers, the debris of Phaethon's chariot.

Hippolytus is obsessed with the cult of Diana, goddess of the moon, hunting, and chastity; he is, in fact, a male Amazon, who rejects women rather than men, despite his apparent love for his mother.

At some point, it is not clear when, Theseus kills Hippolytus' mother, Antiope, and marries Ariadne's sister, Phaedra. Then he goes with his friend Pirithous to carry off Proserpina, the wife of Pluto, god of the dead (and a double for Minos, much as the underworld resembles the labyrinth). The mission is unsuccessful. Pirithous and Theseus are caught and detained in the underworld. When the play begins, Theseus is still absent and Hippolytus is about to go off hunting as the sun rises.

Notes and Questions about the Characters

Hippolytus At the beginning of *Phaedra*, Hippolytus musters his men and his dogs like a military commander dispatching troops; indeed, the final vision in that speech is curiously suggestive of a primitive and gory triumphal parade celebrating man the killer, man the *organized* killer. Hippolytus sees nature in its geographical expanse as the hunter's domain, or rather as his empire. His vision extends beyond Athens and Attica to a far-flung patchwork of peoples, rivers, and mountains at the borders of the Roman world: the Danube, the Don, the Araxes, the Alps, the Pyrenees, Libya, the Arabs, the Scythians (whom I translate as Cossacks). Is there an imperialist inside Hippolytus, this supposed child of nature and the hunt? Compare the play's end, where the tables are turned, where the energy of earth, sea, and land (and the whole force of the mythic past) takes horrendous bull-like form and destroys the huntsman, tears him into pieces and strews him about the landscape.

Is there anything in Hippolytus' opening speech that humanizes or individualizes him? What might make such a person (or what he symbolizes) attractive? Contrast the opening and closing montages of savagery with the way Hippolytus represents his hunter's life to the nurse: an idyllic existence of simple innocence, free from urban corruption. How can we explain these differences? Is Hippolytus more sophisticated than he presents himself as being? He tells the nurse he hates women but is uncertain whether this is a natural reaction, one he has taught himself, or simply rage. He lives, after all, a paradoxical life as a male Amazon.

Note his apparently courteous and sympathetic treatment of Phaedra in the scene immediately following his violent denunciation of women. What is his attitude to Phaedra before she confronts him with her passion for him? The nurse suggests that Hippolytus' hatred of Phaedra is what makes him hate all other women. Is there any possibility that he could be feeling (and repressing) desire for Phaedra? Why is he about to kill her, until her hunger for death by his sword endows the act of killing with a sense of sexual consummation? His casting aside of the sword might suggest a symbolic self-castration, an admission of the proximity of the desire to rape and the desire to kill—as Phaedra's nurse is quick to observe.

Phaedra   In her first speech this daughter of Minos contrasts her father's far-ranging naval power with her own confinement within the house while her husband goes off to rape and fornicate. Does her love for Hippolytus spring from a desire to associate with his freedom of movement and his sexual purity—from what he symbolizes for her rather than what he is? Is her love an attempt to recapture the past? Is Hippolytus really Theseus as he was in younger days, or is this idea simply Phaedra's way of justifying her passion for Hippolytus?

Phaedra seems more obviously aware of her capacity for self-delusion than other characters in the play. She bends her taught morality by talking of the bestial curse upon Cretan women when they love, or the power of the young boy-god, the rather Hippolytus-like Cupid. Phaedra knows as she speaks to Hippolytus that she is putting the wrong construction on his responses but seems prepared to delude herself because this is what she wants to hear. And she vows to pursue him in the underworld even after death. How impossible a goal is this in a play where her husband, Theseus, returns from that very underworld? Or is this *precisely* the ironic problem posed by the mythic scenario: that the rules not only of behavior but of existence apply unevenly?

When Theseus returns from the dead, he finds Phaedra apparently ready to commit suicide. Since at first she adopts a lofty moral tone, we do not know whether she will actually go along with the Nurse's fiction about Hippolytus' attempted rape. Curiously, it is Theseus' threat to torture the Nurse that makes Phaedra "confess." Why? Is this simply a pretext to justify the abandonment of her high moral tone? Or is it her genuine concern for the nurse?

Note the curious change in Phaedra just before she kills herself. The moral tone returns; she sets an example, she says, for Theseus to follow. Yet moments before, in dialogue with herself, she obviously considers (only to dismiss) the possibility of continuing her married sexual relationship with Theseus.

The Nurse A complex and dangerous character who blatantly adopts any rhetorical strategy appropriate to the idea she is selling at a given time, the Nurse argues modesty and moderation to Phaedra yet speaks like a humorously lewd procuress to Hippolytus. Does she despise the vanity of her lords? Does she take it for granted that Hippolytus is really aching to lose his chastity? Notice that she, like Phaedra and Hippolytus, lives in a world which accepts contradictory tenets and paradoxes. Old age, she may claim, gives her freedom to speak her mind; it also makes her lonely and afraid to lose Phaedra (her sole support), however contemptuous she may be of her mistress' vanity. Similarly, she recognizes that Hippolytus' abandoned sword can be construed as evidence not of his raging response to Phaedra's attempted seduction but of a rape. Is the Nurse as lacking in power as her inferior social position seems to suggest?

Theseus Theseus returns to life and to Athens only after Hippolytus has left. Are our initial impressions of him favorable as he reflects on the difficulty of his escape from death? (Notice, by the way, how calmly everyone accepts his return.) His first reactions to Phaedra's plight seem very husbandly and consoling. But then there is a sudden shift: he threatens to torture the nurse. The humane charm is gone and the tyrant emerges. When Phaedra instantly "confesses" she was attacked and, as proof of what happened, gives Theseus the sword Hippolytus left behind, Theseus immediately recognizes the weapon by the crest on it and takes it as evidence that what Phaedra says is true. There is an irony here that the reader unfamiliar with Latin literature may miss.

Theseus may have reason to be suspicious of stepmothers and their jealousies, since he had a particularly murderous stepmother, Medea. Indeed, scholars have long noted that the Senecan description of Hippolytus' sword recalls Ovid's description of Theseus' own sword in *Metamorphoses* 7.419–424. In Ovid, recognition of the sword saves Theseus from being poisoned by his stepmother, Medea: "These poisons Aegeus, his own father—tricked by his wife—offered to his son, as if he were an enemy. Theseus had taken in his unknowing hand the cup given him when his father recognized the family crest on the ivory hilt of his sword and dashed the murderous drink from his lips." In our play, however, Theseus forgets the lesson of his childhood. The sword, a token which saved him from his stepmother, now becomes evidence offered by his son's stepmother which condemns Hippolytus to death.

When Phaedra declares that her suicide is an example for Theseus to follow, Theseus asks the gods to kill him. But (of course) they do not. Yet he does not proceed to suicide as Phaedra does. Why?

CHARACTERS

HIPPOLYTUS	son of Theseus and the Amazon Antiope
PHAEDRA	daughter of Minos, king of Crete, and Pasiphae; wife of Theseus; sister of Theseus' earlier lover, Ariadne; half sister of the Minotaur; stepmother of Hippolytus
THESEUS	king of Athens
NURSE	servant and confidante of Phaedra
MESSENGER	
CHORUS	Athenian people
VARIOUS ATTENDANTS (nonspeaking)	

ACT I

Scene: Athens, shortly before dawn, in front of the royal palace. HIPPO-
LYTUS, *with a group of* ARMED MEN *and packs of hounds, prepares to set
out for the hunt.*

Hippolytus: Move, surround the shaded forest!
                  Over hilltops, fine Athenians,
                  there's no need to stop, so range as
                  far, as fast as you can run. Go
                  where the rocky crags of Parnes
                  glower over lower land, where
                  torrents, tearing Thria's valleys,
                  thrash river banks, mount ridges ever
                  white-capped, aged, mysterious, Balkan.

                  Others, this way where tall alders
                  weave a covering, form a grove. Where
                  virgin meadows nestle, gently   10
                  kissed by Zephyrs, bloom with spring grass
                  as damp dew rises on breezes.
                  There Ilisos' trivial waters
                  lap the slender charms of plowland
                    where seeds, when planted, only shrivel:
                  his thin flow glitters on sand grains.

                  Men, branch left where Marathon bounds
                  open pasture, where wild flocks graze
                  flanked by nursing young at nighttime,
                  creatures small in size and number.

Balkan: Rhipaean mountains

You, go where hard old Acharneus
softens his frigidity, torched
warm below by south winds blowing.   20

You! To honeyed Hymettus' cliffs!
You! Heel down on small Aphidnae!
Sunion's headland, bending sea back,
was too long preserved untouched by
man.
      But if the forest stirs you,
Phlye calls, with wild boar roaming,
terrorizing farmland plowmen,
wanted now for many a wounding.   30

Those are silent hounds, their ropes slack.
Cut them loose. Keep the Dalmatians
back. They're keen. And hold the Cretans.
Fighting-fit, they are. So keep them
chafing collars, straining leashes.

Watch the Spartans. They are headstrong:
hot, like all their breed, for hunting
wildlife. So shorten their leashes.
They'll have chance to make the hollow
caves echo. They're quick to pick up
scents, so now's the time to keep snouts
down to catch what's on the breezes,
sharp noses to ground. For dawn's light   40
fools you.
      Yet the soil is dew–damp
at this hour, and it still holds and
still betrays a footprint's traces.

Someone must bring the wide-mesh netting—
though it's heavy on the neck. Now,

Dalmatians: Molossians

you, the trip-wire loops. Come on, please,
hurry! We need rope, tied up with
feathers—red, to scare our quarry,
corral them into the deathtraps.

You, grip tight a javelin quivering
in your hand, ready for throwing.
This huge pike requires both hands when
you direct its stout blade inwards.   50

Your job is to wait in ambush.
As the beasts run past, stampede them
with your loud cries.
                    Then—it's all yours:
victory's won, so you can take your
crescent flaying-knife, releasing
innards as you slit the belly.

Goddess good as man, be with me.
I am your attentive servant.
You are able to hold power in
realms remote from human creatures,
trace your quarry, loom large over
beasts, hunting with deadly weapons:
beasts that drink the cold Araxes
or play on the frozen Danube.
Further, your spear-hand harasses
lions in the Libyan desert,
does from Crete.
                    You use less force when
your spear-hand pins down the female
as she runs.   60
                    For tigresses with
varied colors nobly face their
breasts towards you. But the bison,

Goddess: Diana

male and shaggy, shows its back. He
flees before you like the wild ox,
though he has great horns upon him.

Any life that grazes lonely
fears your hunting-bow, Diana: 70
Arab in the forest richness,
Berber starving in the desert,
nomad Cossack in no man's Steppes,
Pyrennean mountain hider,
skulker in high Alpine clearings.

If my worship still is pleasing,
I take all your favor with me
when I go into the clearings.
Prey is trapped and safely netted,
feet cannot break free from nooses.
Trophies keep my wagons groaning.
Dogs will redden their sharp noses
steeped in blood; a mob of yokels
head back to their huts in triumph.   80

Goddess, you are with me. I know,
for these hounds keen with shrill baying.
I am called into the woodlands.

I will take the route that shortens
the long way I have to weave.

(*Exeunt* HIPPOLYTUS *and* HUNTSMEN. *Enter* PHAEDRA
from palace, followed by the NURSE.)

Phaedra: Menacing, queenly Crete, your power controls
and bounds water's vastness. Your countless fleet
grips any surface that old Nereus
lets sharp-nosed ships slice through, holds sea and shore
up to Assyria.
                    Why do you force

me, then, to be confined inside a house,
married to your enemy, wasting   90
my life in misery and tears? Theseus,
the fugitive—my husband—is away
again and shows his usual marital
fidelity. Bravely he soldiers on,
through the deep enfolding dark of lakes
that cannot be recrossed. His aim? To help
a rapist lover gain his violent goal:
to tear off from her earthy throne the wife
of Death himself and carry her away.
It is madness, but he allies himself
to it, restrained by neither decency
nor fear.
        So even in the depths of Hell,
he hunts for fornication or the chance
to rape, this father of Hippolytus.
But there's another and more ghastly pain
that presses down upon me in my grief.
I get no rest at night, find no release
from my anxiety in heavy sleep.   100
Evil grows deep and large in me, erupts
and scalds like a volcano's smoky waves.
The loom Athena made for wives is now
empty; threads elude my weaving hands.
I find no pleasure in making temples
splendid with votive gifts, or in joining
Athenian girls at ceremonial dance
among the altars and tossing torches
which have known the touch of rituals
we should never discuss. Nor do I like
to make my way, in chastity of prayer,
in purity of rite, to the divine
presidency of her who was adjudged
this land of law and order as her realm.

---

a rapist lover: Pirithous
rituals: see Eleusis
presidency: see Pallas

My delight would be arousing beasts
to run, pursuing them, tossing stiff spears
in my soft hand.
      Now you are running wild,
good mind. What is this love, this urge to leap   110
into forest clearings?
        I recognize
the deadly inner fruit that lures me as
it lured my pitiful mother. Our love
has heard its instincts sinfully evoked
within the wood. Woman who gave me birth,
I pity you. You were ravished with lust
for the bestial lord of a wild herd.
You were daring, and you fulfilled your love.
Oh, he was bullish, your adulterer,
and hated any mated partnership.
He was leader of flocking animals
untamed. But nonetheless he fell in love
with what it was he saw.
       Does any god
or Daedalus have power to satisfy   120
the fire within me? I need pity too.
And yet, if Daedalus came back—this man
who locked within the darkness of our home
the monster we had made—he still could not,
with all his potency of Attic art,
promise me help in my catastrophe.
Venus will not look upon the Sun,
for Love hates daylight's children such as I;
through us she gains her vengeance for the chains
that coupled her to Mars and War. She loads
all Phoebus' relatives with shameful lust.
Minos' daughters never consummate
a trivial affair. And when they mate,
they always sin against all decency.

---

that coupled her to Mars: Phoebus Apollo had mocked Venus when her husband, Vulcan,
caught her in adultery with Mars.

Nurse: You are the wife of Theseus and you are
of brilliant ancestry, from Jupiter
himself. Keep your heart chaste. Quick as you can,
shake out indecency and sin. And quench   130
its flames. Don't just follow obediently
or harbor this sin even as a hope.
Stand firm against love's first attack. You'll win,
you'll drive it back, be safe. Its fruit is sweet
yet bad. If you are soft and nourish it,
you'll doom yourself to unconditional
surrender and humiliating loss.
(*These next lines may either be addressed to* PHAEDRA *or spoken as an aside.*)
It does not escape me, I should add,
that royal vanity, unused to truth,
hardens itself in swollen self-esteem,
has no wish to be bent towards justice.
But I will run whatever risk there is,
and take what fate allots. Why? I am old
and freedom is at hand. That makes me brave.

The best way to live honestly is this:
to want to do so and stick to the path   140
without slipping. The second best is this:
to be shamed into knowing the limits
to place upon the beast lurking within.
But, pitiable woman, what of you?
Your family's notorious enough.
You make things worse, your deeds amount to more
than what your mother did. Your conscious sin
surpasses her monstrous obsessiveness.
The monstrous can be termed a freak of fate,
an act of god. But sinful crimes suggest
some personal failure of morality.
If you suppose you can sin yet be safe,
and do not have to cower in fear because
your husband cannot see what's happening

in the world above, *you* are the one
who's lost and wandering.
                                    Suppose Theseus
is dungeoned in chains and plunged in deep
oblivion, that he must now endure
death and the Styx for all eternity.
What of your father? His authority
extends far and is law for people in
a hundred cities. He controls the seas.   150
Will he allow crime such as yours to go
unseen and undetected? Parents are
shrewd as well as anxious.
                                    Still, suppose
that we, despite its magnitude, conceal
this sin by some sophisticated trick,
there's your maternal grandfather to face.
He pours his light on everything there is.

And there's the father of the gods himself,
who shakes the universe and brandishes
in his bright hand the bolts of lightning forged
in pure volcanic fire. Considering
that your grandparents see everything,
do you suppose you can devise a plan
that will elude their eyes?
                                    But then again—

What if the gods are with you, favor you?
Say they give cover as you mate in sin,
that, as you fornicate, they really do   160
keep safe your secret—though in the real world
we know such things don't happen when great crimes
occur. There's still something to penalize
you which won't be dislodged. I mean the mind,
the terror of knowing, the soul teeming

---

grandfather: Sol
father of the gods: Jupiter

with guilt and frightened even of itself.
How do you deal with that?
                        Some women have
stayed safe though they have sinned, but none has kept
anxiety at bay.
                 I beg you, then,
smother the flames of your incestuous love.
Don't filthy yourself with sin savages
have yet to consummate. Nomad Getae
upon the plains avoid incest. So do
men from the Taurus, Bull Mountain people,
who hate outsiders, and the Cossacks too
who live in isolated, scattered groups.

Your mind can purge itself. From it you must
expel all thought of this perverted act.

Remember your mother and be afraid
of such aberrant sexuality.   170
Do you propose to bed father and son,
conceive a fetus from the sperm of both
in your incestuous womb?
                   Go on, reverse
the basic laws of natural birth with your
obscene passion! Why not let monsters thrive?
You leave your brother's princely halls unfilled—
What kind of cowardly neglect is this?
The world will hear of prodigies unknown,
nature will bend its reproductive laws,
each time a Cretan woman loves.

Phaedra: I know,
dear nurse, that what you say is true. You're right.
But passion forces me to follow down
the path I know is worse. My soul does grasp
what's happening, hunts sane advice. In vain.

---

your brother's princely halls: the Minotaur's labyrinth

It still races towards the precipice. 180
My life is like the sailor's who urges
his loaded ship head on to heavy seas.
His work comes to nothing. The steering deck
is overwhelmed, washed level by the waves.
What power has guiding reason? Victory
goes to the passions, they're now in control,
their potent god is master of my mind.

He is the winged force of potency
throughout the universe. And when he strikes
his fire savages Jupiter himself.
There is no cure. The warrior god, crushing
life under his heel, is seared and burns.
The smith who forges jagged lightning bolts,
who copes eternally with Aetna's heat,
impassioned furnaces, volcanic fire, 190
grows hot when love's minute flame takes its hold.
Phoebus, himself a master of tense strings
and shafts, is pierced by love's more accurate
arrow.
          Indeed, this lightly-fluttering boy
makes heavy impact on both earth and heaven.

Nurse: Lust in its craving for debauchery
invented the idea of love as god.
It gave passion this fake divinity,
this title of respectability,
so it could be freer to rove at will.

Hence the myth that Venus sends her son
to wander all around the earth, the myth
that he flies through the heavens, brandishing
his horny weapons in his tender hand, 200

---

potent god: Amor
warrior god: Gradivus
the smith: Vulcan

hence the paradox that a tiny god
should have such massive power.

Intelligence
gone mad devised these mad inanities
to suit itself, made a divinity
of venereal love, fashioned the god,
fashioned his bow.

Now anyone who lives
high in excessive affluence, wallows
in constant streams of luxury, always
hungers and hunts for the unusual.
Then lust, ever the bad companion
of great success, slips in. Banquets become
routine and boring; so does ordinary
wine, buildings of reasonable size.

Why does this menace slip less frequently
into the poor man's house, choosing instead
discriminating homes? And why is sex   210
held so scrupulously sacrosanct
in small houses, why do the middle ranks
among us keep emotions within healthy
bounds? Do modest means make moderate lives?
The rich, in contrast, levered up by power,
seem to be hunting more than is decent
and right. Give someone too much power, and he
wants to control what lies beyond his power.
You see and know what is decent conduct
for a woman who occupies a throne.
Fear your husband's authority, for he
is king. Respect it.

He *is* coming home.

Phaedra: I think love is my greatest ruling lord;
the other won't come back. No fear of that.
Once someone has sunk into endless night,
entered the house of darkness, he cannot
touch what is in this world above again.   220

Nurse: Don't bank on Death's reliability.
              True, he may lock his vaults and guard the doors,
              secure enough themselves, with a watchdog
              of the dead. But Theseus *is* your one
              exception. He finds paths that don't exist.

Phaedra: He will, perhaps, come to forgive my love.

Nurse: Not he. This man was savage even to
              a faithful wife. Antiope—foreign,
              used to ruthlessness—found him a brute.
              But say you can soften your husband's wrath.
              Who'll soften the son's rebellious soul?
              Name something female—loathing emanates
              from him, he runs away. He vows himself   230
              to lifelong celibacy, he steers clear
              of celebrating his own wedding day.
              A beast, that's what he is. In temperament
              you'd recognize him as an Amazon.

Phaedra: I'll follow him into the high forests,
              across the mountains. That is my desire.
              I don't care if he clings to rockfaces
              on snowcapped bluffs or if his agile feet
              find jagged boulders underneath their heels.

Nurse: You think he'll stop and yield to your fondling,
              that he'll strip off habits of chastity
              not just for sex, but incest? You'll make him stop
              hating women, you think? The chances are
              his hate for you turns him against the rest.
              He can't be overcome by coaxing prayers.

Phaedra: He is a beast. But I've learned love subdues
              the beast.   240

Nurse: He'll run from you.

Phaedra: I'll follow him,
even if he runs across oceans.

Nurse: Think of your father...

Phaedra: I think of mother too.

Nurse: He entirely shuns the female sex.

Phaedra: Then there'll be no rivals. He'll be just mine.

Nurse: Your husband will arrive...

Phaedra: Pirithous'
fellow rapist...

Nurse: Your father will arrive.

Phaedra: He's fine. He's Ariadne's father too.

Nurse: I'm old. Respect the white hair on my head.
I've tired myself with worries about you.
My breasts fed you. Now, on my knees, I beg:
control your passion. Try to help yourself.
Wanting a cure is part of getting well.

Phaedra: My conscience has not lost all sense of shame.   250
You brought me up, and I'll do as you say.
A love that does not want to be reined in
can be subdued.
                         People speak well of me,
and I won't have my reputation stained.
From this dilemma there's one lone escape,
one sole recourse to which reason may turn.

He's fine: Phaedra argues that Minos will not be angry with her because he hates
Theseus for his treatment of his other daughter

Let me go to my husband, cease to live.
My death can then prevent a perverse sin.

Nurse:　　Your impulses, your mind, need some control.
Let me help you. Keep the bridle on
your wild spirits. I testify on oath
that you deserve to live since you have passed
this sentence of death upon yourself.

Phaedra:　　It is decreed! The Cretan dies! But how?
The mode of death must be determined now.
Shall I hang or shall I fall upon
a sword or leap from the acropolis?　　　　　260

Nurse:　　How can I, in my old age, let you
destroy yourself like this, leap to your death?
This impulse is pure madness. Stop it now.
No one can come back from the dead—with ease.

Phaedra:　　No reasoning has power to prevent
the death of someone who decides to die
and ought to die. To guard and, yes, avenge
my chastity, I will now take up arms.

Nurse:　　My lady, I am old, tired, and alone.
You are my life's sole consolation now.
If lust and passion are so embedded
inside your mind, forget what people say.
When people talk, they're not after the truth.
They're good to people who deserve much worse.
But they'll malign you if you're really good.　　　270

He has a glowering stubbornness of mind,
but let's probe it. It will then be my task
to beard the youthful beast, to flex and bend
his fierce mind. He is savage—and a man.

(*Exeunt* NURSE *and* PHAEDRA *into palace. Enter*
CHORUS.)

Chorus: Goddess, your power is   spawned in savage sea swirl;
           Cupid's twin forces,   obsession and revulsion,
           call you their mother.   Glistening and lustful,
           that wicked boy with   taut, unerring bowstring
           controls his weapons,   all that makes him potent
           both in his shafts and   in the fires they kindle.

           His passion slithers   into each bone's hollow,
           thieflike its fire lays   waste the veins it comes to.   280
           When he strikes blows they   leave no obvious gashes
           yet penetrate deep   into hidden hollows.

           That boy allows no   peace, but nimbly scatters
           his shafts and sprays them   throughout all creation.
           Every land knows the   pulsing of his torment:
           shores facing day's birth,   or its western turnpost,
           lands seething under   the Tropic of Cancer,
           lands freezing under   the cold Arctic Circle
           where human settlers   wander, never settling.   290
           He stirs the fierceness   of youth's flames to furnace,
           pokes heat into tired   senility's dead embers,
           fans and ignites hearts   ignorant and virgin,
           orders the gods to   leave the heavens above us
           and live on earth in   intentional disguises.

           In Thessaly Phoebus   became a drover,
           rounded up herds and   set aside his zither
           called home the cattle   with a rustic's reedpipes.

           Even the god who   crafted sky and rainclouds
           often assumes forms   that are far beneath him.   300

Goddess: Venus
wicked boy: Cupid
god who crafted sky: Jupiter

He plummets down now   in his wan white plumage,
his voice beguiling   more than dying swan's song.

Now he's more torrid,   like a horny bullock,
lowers his back to   let the virgins play there,
swims in the waves of   his brother's sea waters,
an alien realm. There,   he uses his new-hoofed feet,
sweeps them like slow oars,   tames the deep-poured
        ocean,
chest boldly breasting   swell, and yet afraid for
his plundered cargo,   pirated for swift rape.

She too, bright goddess   of celestial darkness,
finds herself burning,   abandons her own nighttime,
leaving her lunar   course to solar brother
who guides its movement   in a different manner.   310

He learns to drive the   chariot of nighttime
but steers it in a   closer, tighter orbit
while axles shudder   from a heavier burden.

Night does not keep to   its appointed limits.
Day returns slowly   to its new arising.

Hercules, born of   Alcmena, discarded
his deadly arrows,   and the threatening hide he'd
stripped from a huge and   devastating lion.
He let his fingers   be bejeweled with emeralds,
and let his wild hair   be combed into order,
wore golden stockings   on his calves, and cramped his 320
feet into yellow   shoes. His hand that wielded
a knotted club   spun threads on flying spindles.

Persia and Lydia   ripe in their riches
observed the hide of   rapacious lion

---

like a horny bullock: Europa
bright goddess: Diana
solar brother: Sol, Phoebus

cast down to earth.
Over those shoulders   on which once rested
great Heaven's palace   now fluttered lightly
Tyrian threads.

This fire is god—believe us, it's hurt us—   330
it is too potent.   Where the deep salt sea
circles the landmass,   where the white stars course
on through the clear void,   there rules the power of
the savage boy. His   pointed shafts are sensed
in bottommost pools   by bluish shoals of
Nereid mermaids.   Sea cannot cool the
fire of their fever.
                    Creatures with wings sense
the Fire's force of burning.   Goaded by Venus
bullocks are boldened   to beauty of battle,
fighting for whole herds.   340
                    And timid stags, when
fearing lost stud-rights,   challenge to combat.

At mating time all   India's bronzed folk
fear the striped tiger;   boars sharpen hard tusks,
made to inflict wounds,   foam coats their hot mouths.

Lions of Carthage   shake their maned necks and
greet in their roaring   the onset of their
passion for mating.
                    And when Love moves them,
whole forests groan with   bestial bellowing.   350
Love strikes the monsters   of the mad ocean,
even bull-elephants.
                    He claims all nature.
Nothing escapes him,   for, when Love bids it,
hatred must wither,   vendettas give ground to
his searing fires. So: What further example
can my song offer?   Love's gnawing care tames
cruel stepmothers.

ACT II

NURSE *enters from palace.*

Chorus: Nurse, tell us your tale. Where is the queen?
Is there some sign that her passion abates?

Nurse: There is no hope that suffering as great
as hers can be allayed. Nothing can halt   360
the raging fire searing, consuming her.
She does not talk about it. No, she keeps
it locked within herself. Yet what she wants,
however much she would dissemble it,
betrays itself in her expressive face.
Fire bursts out from her eyes; her cheeks look tired
and cannot stand the light. She vacillates,
never approves the same thing twice. Her pain,
not knowing where to send her, tosses her
this way and that. One moment she staggers,
faints as if dying, as if she could
hardly hold her head straight on her neck.
The next moment she tries to get herself
to rest, but spends the night sleepless, in tears.   370
She has them prop her up then lay her down;
remove her ribbons, do her hair again.
Unable to endure the way she looks,
she changes her dress constantly. Her health
does not concern her; neither does her food.
Her feet move aimlessly, her strength is gone.
She now lacks her old energy. The bright
color that rouged her natural radiance
is gone. Concern cripples her joints and limbs,
she walks unsteadily; her body, once
magnetic in its radiant allure,

has lost its beauty, and her eyes that shone
with all the brilliance of sun and moon
show nothing of their ancestry of fire.   380
Incessant tears stream, an erosive dew
canyoning her cheeks like the warm rain
which, when it strikes the yokelike ridges high
in the Bull Mountains, pits and melts the snow.
(*The palace doors open, revealing* PHAEDRA *lying on her*
couch.)
But now the palace doors are opening.
See, she is lying on her gilded bed,
refusing to put on her usual clothes.
She is no longer fully rational.

Phaedra: Maids, take away these royal, purple robes,
this cloth woven with gold. I want nothing
to do with the red blush of Tyrian dye,
or silk threads cropped from distant Chinese trees.
Give me a narrow belt in which to tuck
my skirts. I want my neck free of pendants;   390
I'll have no white pearl earrings, sparkling gifts
from Indian seas. My hair too must be free,
unsprayed with perfumes from Assyria.
Let it flow down my neck, tossed as it will,
till it brushes my shoulders, till it blows
behind me in the breezes as I run.
The left hand holds the quiver. And the right
should brandish a Thessalian thrusting spear.
Harsh Hippolytus! His mother looked
like this when she once left the shores and ice
of the Black Sea, a woman from the Don
or the Maeotis, who then drove her hordes
thundering onto Athenian soil.
She drew her hair into a single knot   400
and let it hang. A moonlike, crescent shield
guarded her side. And that is how I too
will go wildly into the forest's depths.

Chorus: Now stop this! Nothing is made easier
           by wallowing in your pain and misery.
           Pray to the virgin goddess of the fields,
           placate the power of her divinity.

Nurse: Queen of woodlands, living in solitude
           upon the hills, sole female deity
           alive in solitary hills, alter
           your omens' meaning; make them less grimly
           menacing. Goddess so powerful
           in forest and in clearing, brilliant star
           of heaven, glory of the night whose gleam,   410
           waxing and waning, lights the universe:
           I call upon your three forms, Hecate.
           Be with me now and bless what I would do.
           Tame fierce Hippolytus and civilize
           his rigid qualities. Open his ears,
           soften his wildness. Better he learn sweet love,
           and share bewildered passion. Trap his mind.
           Though strong-willed, hostile, beastlike, let him come
           under the laws of Venus. Use raw force
           to the full. And in return, I pray
           your shining face may bear you where you will,
           that your pure horns may penetrate the veil
           of bridling clouds. May no witch have the power
           to drag you down with spells from Thessaly
           as you control the reins of heaven at night.   420
           And may no shepherd brag that you are his.
           Goddess, I called you. Come, and grant my prayer.
           (*Enter* HIPPOLYTUS, *unattended*.)
           I see Hippolytus approaching now
           to venerate his goddess solemnly.
           No one stands at his side.
                                    Why hesitate?
           The time and place come as a gift of chance.
           Deploy your skills.
                                    Why am I trembling so?
           It is not easy to work up courage

to do a crime you have been told to do.
But if one is afraid of royal commands,
one must reshape one's thoughts, expel all hope
of high standing at court. A good conscience
makes for a bad servant of royal will. 430

Hippolytus: Why do you come to see me, faithful nurse?
It's hard for you to move, you're tired and old.
Your forehead frets, your face is sad. Why so?
My father's well, I trust? Is Phaedra well?
And what about the twins? Are they alright?

Nurse: Be free from fear. The royal house is well,
in fact, it prospers, flowers, gains new strength
and fruitfulness. But you yourself should come
more gently into this Elysian state.

When fate leaves you no choice, such misery
may come to be excused. But any man 440
who dedicates himself to suffering
by his own choice, and flagellates himself,
deserves to lose the good things that he has
but is too ignorant to use.
So think.
There are alternatives. You're young, relax
your mind. Nights are for revels. Take a torch.
Let Bacchus lift the dead weight of your cares.
Enjoy youth, it is racing from you now.
Your heart will not refuse. For youths exude
their sexuality. Your spirit throbs.
Why lie still and alone upon your bed?

Sell off your youthful gloom, set sail, pirate
the luxuries, cast off hawsers, forbid 450
the best days of your life to flow past you!
God has so written: that each age of man

---

the twins: Phaedra's two children by Theseus were Acamas and Demophon.

shall have its special task. And he conducts
us through them, step by step. Joy suits the youth,
sad faces suit old men. Instinct is good
and natural. Why should you strangle it?
Why contain yourself?
                              The farmer gains
most profit from the crop which while still green
is prodigal, surges up happily.
A high-topped tree will tower above its grove
unless malicious hands would cut it down
or prune it back.
                              The upright intellect
better advances its own claim to praise
if freedom livens, feeds its noble soul.   460

Must you live ignorant of life, a crude
eccentric woodsman, vowed to youthful gloom,
ascetic sexlessness? Is it decreed,
you think, that men must offer themselves up
to live rough, break in horses on the run,
and fight in vicious wars steeped in Mars' blood?
there are so many different kinds of death
tugging at the crowds of mortal men,
picking them off! Sea, sword, and treachery.
Yet even if such deaths did not occur,
we'd head on by ourselves towards dark Styx.

The mighty parent of the universe
discerned the sheer rapacity of Fate
and so provided that losses to death
should always be replaced by new issue.
Venus, sexuality, makes up,
restores the race that threatens to run dry.   470

But what if she were gone? The earth will rot,
lie motionless; the empty sea stand still,
no fish within her. There will be no bird

up in the sky, no creature in the woods.
Only the winds will travel through the air.

Say, then, our youth declines to reproduce,
praises the life of chastity. This age,
the one you see, will be the sum total
of everything. The world will die with it.   480
Nature should, therefore, guide your life and you
should follow. Go to the city frequently;
live intimately with the people there.

Hippolytus: There is no other way of life more free,
less wayward, nurturing values and rites
from olden days, than that which quits cities
and loves the wilds. Passions, greed mad of mind,
never sear the man who dedicates
himself to mountains and to innocence.
No demagoguery, no vulgar spite
for the elite, no deadly, spying hate,
no fragile patronage can hurt him there.
He neither schemes for power nor is its slave,   490
pursuing hollow honors or the tides
of wealth. He's free from fear; he's also free
from hope. Dark, gnawing envy cannot get
its debased, rotting fangs into his throat.
Corruption, sown where populations teem
and cities swell, is all unknown to him.
He is not keyed, in terror, to each noise;
he does not lie, he does not yearn to sleep
richly beneath a thousand-columned roof.
He does not have the arrogance to plate
his ceiling rafters with thick layers of gold,
or drown god's altars in a sea of blood
and have a hundred snow-white oxen give
their necks to ritual sacrament and death.   500
His realm of power is empty pastureland,
the open skies. He lives a nomad's life,

and does no harm. The only cunning traps
that he knows how to set are for wild game.
The work is hard. When tired, he revives
his body in the snow-chilled Ilisos.
Sometimes he hunts along swift Alpheus' banks.
Sometimes he works his way across dense bush
in tall clumps through which Lerna's ice-cold stream
glistens shallow and crystalline: places
to sit in silence, places where birds trill
plaintive, chaotic song and where ash groves
and ancient beeches, gently wind-strummed, thrill.
His pleasure: to recline upon the banks   510
of a meandering stream, catnap lightly
on damp, naked turf where waterfalls
thunder into profundity, or where
the sweet sounds of a rushing rivulet
murmur among newly blooming flowers.

He shakes the woodland apple tree for fruit
to tame his hunger, culls wild strawberries
from tiny clusters: food easy to hand
for modest needs. Imperial luxury
he shuns instinctively. The arrogant
shudder when they drink from gold, but he
tingles with pleasure as, with his bare hands,
he cups springwater. Though his bed is hard,
sleep presses deeply, his limbs totally   520
relax. His is no hidden bedroom that
lacks light but not anxiety and guilt
where he schemes like a thief. And he does not
bury himself in fear inside a house
built like a labyrinth. He yearns for light,
for open air; he is alive, standing
before heaven undisguised.
                              I think
the first life nature poured in human mold
was touched by the divine and lived like this.
It felt no blinding lust for gold; it set

no consecrated stone on open plain
to sit in judgment, mark out for the eye
whose fields were whose. And speculative ships 530
did not yet scar the sea. Men knew only
waters close to home. No vast ramparts
thick with turrets girded city flanks.
No soldiers trained their hands to skill at arms.
Gates were not closed, torqued catapults did not
cannon heavy rocks to break them down.
Earth had not yet been ordered to endure
an overlord and the vile servitude
of coupled bulls plowing upon her soil.
Fields reproduced the crops all by themselves.
Nations were fed without the need to ask
or fear. The wilds produced wealth naturally
and gave it freely, as the sheltering caves
provided natural housing for mankind.

Passion for personal gain at any cost 540
smashed down this covenant. Unstoppable
anger abetted, as did lust which sets
the mind on fire and goads men on. Next came
the thirst, bloodthirst, for power. Then the big
began to prey upon the small and weak;
rights won by raw strength were scrawled into law.
They warred, at first barefisted, then they shaped
a rock, or formless wood's bulk, as a club.
As yet the slender shaft of cornel-wood
armed with thin tempered steel was not at hand;
no saber with long blade hung at men's sides,
no helmets, hair-crested, enhanced their height.
Grievances kept forging weapons. Mars,
obsessed with war, designed thousands of new 550
forms and instruments of death. Blood spread
from these beginnings, staining all the earth,
making the sea blush red. All boundaries
were washed away, crime ripped through families,
every wicked permutation found

exemplars: brother kills brother, father
kills son, husband's throat is cut by wife,
mothers unnaturally execute
the children they have borne. And stepmothers—
I say no more: they're worse than animals.
Women lead us in evil. Engineers
of crime, they lay siege to our minds, leave us
obsessed. Because of them, cities are burned   560
in thousands, nations engage in countless wars,
kingdoms are depeopled and wiped out.
No need to mention others when just one
will mark the whole of womankind as damned:
Medea, wife of the deceased Aegeus.

Nurse: A few committed crimes. Why blame us all?

Hippolytus: I shun, I flee, I cut you from my life,
I curse the lot of you. Perhaps it is
nature—or perhaps I've taught myself.
Perhaps it is blind rage. But hating you
affords me pleasure, and you will couple
fire to water, uncertain Syrtes   570
will open up a passageway for ships
through maelstrom swirl, Tethys will make day rise
within her western lap, the mouths of wolves
shall cease to threaten deer before my will
is overcome, softens to woman's wiles.

Nurse: Love often bridles those who hold out hard,
muting and changing hate. Your mother—think
about the fierce women she ruled. They feel
the coupling force of Venus. You attest
to it: the only boy-child of your race.

Hippolytus: The only consolation I have had
for mother's death is that it lets me hate
all women, without one exception.

Nurse:	Like granite headland, so unwavering 580

Like granite headland, so unwavering   580
against the waves he stands, hurls back breakers
that would smash it. He spits upon my words.
(*Enter* PHAEDRA, *distraught and on the point of fainting.*)
But Phaedra rushes to the edge. She can't
endure delay. Which way will fortune turn?
What will her obsession drive her to?
(PHAEDRA *faints;* HIPPOLYTUS *rushes to her side.*)
She's fallen to the ground, her body seems
lifeless. The gray of death shows on her face.
(*She moves over to* PHAEDRA *and joins* HIPPOLYTUS *in an
effort to bring her round.*)
Show your will to live! Please find the power
to speak, my child. Look, your Hippolytus
is using his own arms to hold you up.

Phaedra: Who is it brings me back to pain, restores
the seething torment of my mind? How good
it was to lose all sense of self, of me.   590

Hippolytus: Daylight is sweet. It is a gift regained.
Why do you want to run away from it?

Phaedra: (*inwardly*)
Be audacious, mind, and carry through
on what you want to do. Your words must be
fearless and resolute. Ask timidly
and you'll invite rebuff. The major part
of this crime has been done a long time since.
It is too late for chastity. I've loved
a sinful love. And if I carry through
on what I've started, maybe I'll bury
all slanders, torch them with wedding fires.
Success, by tortuous logic, might convert
crime to respectability. So start!
(*to* HIPPOLYTUS)
Please come aside and listen for a while.
Have anyone who's with you go away.   600

71

Hippolytus: There's no one. You may speak without restraint.

Phaedra: The words start, but my mouth won't let them pass.
A great force prompts my voice; a greater force
restrains it. Powers of heaven, I testify
before you: what I want I do not want.

Hippolytus: Your mind desires something but cannot speak?

Phaedra: Anxieties, when slight, one can express
in words; when great, they stand dumbly silent.

Hippolytus: Trust your anxieties to me, mother.

Phaedra: Mother. A proud and overwhelming name.
Some name more down to earth fits how I feel.   610
Call me your sister, or call me your maid,
Hippolytus. Maid is what I'd prefer.
There is no service I'll not render you.
If you told me to go through drifts of snow
I would not hesitate to walk the peaks
of icy Pindus, and if you told me
to go through fire, through ranks of enemies,
I would immediately offer my breast
to swords unsheathed. Take the authority
that I was left, and take me as your maid:
it's right that you should rule and I obey.
Women do not control, keep cities safe.
You, the flower of youthful energy,   620
can rule the citizens. Your father's power
will give you strength. Take me, your suppliant slave,
to your bosom; protect and cover me.
Pity this widow.

Hippolytus: Almighty god
Let there be nothing in that word you said!
May father come back both safe and soon!

Phaedra: Death is a state that lets nobody out.
The Stygian world is silent, and its lord
makes no return roadway for those who leave
the world above. Will he send back the man
who raped his wife? No, not unless Pluto
sits back complacently and yields to love.

Hippolytus: The gods deal justly, so they'll lead him back.
But while the deity makes up his mind   630
to grant us his release, I will attend
to my dear brothers as a good man should,
and I will work at making you forget
your thoughts of widowhood. I will myself
take up my father's place, fulfill his role.

Phaedra: (*inwardly*)
How readily lovers believe! And Love,
how you deceive us! He has said enough.
I'll marshall my entreaties and advance.
Pity me, and hear, spoken aloud,
the prayers that run in silence through my mind.
I yearn to speak them, but I am ashamed.

Hippolytus: Tell me, what is the evil troubling you?

Phaedra: An evil that you would hardly believe
could ever fall upon a stepmother.

Hippolytus: You're tossing words about all intertwined,
ambiguous in tone. Speak openly.

Phaedra: My heart is mad, seared by the heat of love.   640
Fierce fire, plunged deep inside me, lurks and seethes,
coursing through my veins as dancing flames
penetrate the inner rings of wood.

Hippolytus: This love you rage and burn with, I take it,
is proper for a wife, is for Theseus?

73

Phaedra: Hippolytus. This, then, is how it is.
I love Theseus' face—the way it looked
in years gone by, when he was still a boy,
when the first trace of beard gave character
to his pure cheeks, and when he saw the house
at Cnossos, built to hide a monstrous sight
from human eyes, and when he gathered up
the long thread in the curving labyrinth.   650
Oh, how it shone! His hair was kempt and taut
in priestly bands, a tawny touch of blush
tinged his tender face. His arms were soft,
but muscles were embedded deep in them.
He looked like your Phoebe, or my Phoebus,
or rather like yourself. That's it—the way
he looked when he so charmed his foe. Just so—
his head was high. Your beauty shines like his,
but less self-consciously.

                Still, he's all there,
your father. And part of your fierce mother
blends in a beauty no less thoroughbred:
a Greek face with some stiffer, Cossack lines.   660
Had you sailed with your father into Crete
my sister would have spun her thread for you
in preference. O sister, I don't know
where in the sky you shine, but I beg you
to help me in my plight; we are a pair.
One house has ravished, ruined two sisters:
the father took you; now the son takes me.
(PHAEDRA *kneels in front of* HIPPOLYTUS.)
See: the offspring of a royal house
lies prostrate at your knees, my only lapse
from chastity and innocence. The change
is due to you. I stoop to beg, knowing
what this involves. This day will either

O sister: Ariadne

sear my pain or sear my life away.
Pity my love.   670

Hippolytus: Great ruler of the gods!
Crime moves so swiftly, and you are so slow
to hear, to see. When will your ruthless hand
hurl down its thunderbolts if it is idle
now? Sunlight is stunned by darkness, day
bridled with black clouds, the stars turn back.
Titan, radiant Sun, head crowned with stars,
can you not see your granddaughter's vile sin?
Plunge down, take refuge in the grip of night!
Just ruler of gods and men, why
is your good hand unarmed, why does the world   680
not blaze with firebrands, serpent tongues of flame?
Thunder against me, pierce me with lightning,
let racing fire course through me, burn me up!
I am guilty, I have earned such death.
For I aroused my stepmother's desire.
Was I a fit choice for adultery?
Did I seem to you the sole easy
material to work your crime? Is this
the ruinous payoff for my uprightness?
Oh, you outclass the female sex in crime,
stepping beyond the bestiality
in which your mother so excelled. At least
she filthied and debauched only herself.
Nor did she talk about her guilt until   690
the hybrid child she bore, half man, half beast,
showed the world in its fierce face the crime
its mother did. And in that same womb you
were born.
                    O three and four times blessed are men,
how lucky is their doom, when plots and hate
devour them, suck them down, do them to death!
Father, I envy you. My stepmother
is far more evil than Medea was.

Phaedra: I know our royal house, its cursed fate.
We hunt what we should shun. But I have no
control over myself; I'll follow you
even through fire and across raging sea,   700
boulder, and torrent-ravished river-stream.
Where you step, love's delirium will drive
me too. Once more, proud man, it prostrates me
upon the ground before you, at your feet.

Hippolytus: Take your hands away from me. Their filth
pollutes my purity. And now you dare
to run into my arms? I'll draw my sword,
exact the price your whorish prayer demands.
I twist the hair upon your filthy head
with my left hand. O goddess of the hunt,
never was blood more justly offered you.
(HIPPOLYTUS *draws his sword and is about to stab*
PHAEDRA.)

Phaedra: Hippolytus, you consummate my dreams,   710
cure my madness. Yet in my wildest dreams
I never thought I'd loose my soul in death
beneath your grip, yet keep my chastity.

Hippolytus: Then go away and live. I will deny
your wish. My sword, contaminated by
your touch, I cast away from my chaste thigh.
What river Don is there to wash me clean,
what Maeotis, with waters surging out
into the Black Sea? Neptune's whole ocean
could not purge out the stain of such a crime.
Let me go back to woodlands and wild beasts!
(HIPPOLYTUS *runs offstage, leaving his sword behind.*)

Nurse: Her guilty secret's out. Think quickly, mind—
don't be so dense and slow. It is our job
to reconstrue this outrage so it will

appear as his incestuous passion, not   720
as hers. A wrongful act must cover up
a wrongful act. When an attack is feared,
the safest course is to strike first oneself.
Her guilt was secretly avowed. No one
can testify this vile initiative
was ours. We could be victims of a crime.

Men of Athens, trusted servants, here!
Help! Hippolytus is intent on rape,
on a vile sexual assault! He's here,
and he's upon us, threatening death!
The sword is terrifying her, but she
resists.
       Thank god! He's panicked, rushed away
and dropped his sword! We have the evidence!
But first, revive her! She is faint with shock.   730
Her hair's disheveled, some has been torn out.
No, keep it as it is—still further proof
of what he did! Take her on into town.
(*going over to* PHAEDRA, *who has run, sobbing, to the palace
door*)
Collect your wits, my queen, don't harm yourself,
don't rush out of our sight! Just remember:
shame is a state of mind, not of events.

(*Enter* CHORUS.)

Chorus: He ran like a raging hurricane before us,
like a nor'wester spinning clouds but faster,
faster than stellar comet racked with flames,
driven by winds, extending far in its wake
a fiery trailpath.   740
(*Either the* CHORUS *leaves the* NURSE *and* PHAEDRA *to
their own devices at this point, or* PHAEDRA *and the* NURSE
withdraw into the palace.)
Fame tends to favor   things of bygone ages,
but when compared with   you all ancient glory

77

fades. For your beauty   outshines other brightness
as moon outshines stars   when, circle completed,
when, as her horns join   in a fiery roundness,
Phoebe runs nightlong   in her rapid orbit,
shows just a trace of   blushing on her fair face,
and stars lose grip on   their less brilliant torches.
Like evening starlight   introducing darkness,
angel of nighttime,   fresh washed in the ocean;   750
like morning star,   when grasp of night is broken,
angel of daylight.

You, from pine-carrying   peoples of India,
Bacchus, perpetually   long-haired and young-looking,
terror of tigers with   vine-covered javelin.
Your turban taming a   head crowned with oxen-horns
can't even vie with the   hair of Hippolytus.
Don't take too flattering a   view of your own good
      looks.
Word is round everywhere   that Phaedra's sister once
had, and preferred to have,   Theseus to you, Bacchus. 760

Beauty for mortals is good and bad:
a gift—but brief; its time but short.
Her foot so fleet, so quick her fall.

I won't compare meadows,   true green in springtime,
ravaged by heat-haze   of searing summers
when high sun stands still,   cruel at noonday,
when rapid night hurtles   short-wheeled, tight-circling.

As lilies, pale-petaled,   languidly shrivel,
so gorgeous tresses thin   drily on our heads.
The striking radiance,   the sheen of young cheeks— 770
erased in an instant.   Each passing day's light
spoils, erodes partially,   beauty of body.
For beauty is matter,   fugitive nature.
What wise man banks upon   things that must wither?

Use them while they blossom.   Tacit time saps you.
Bad hours wearied you;   worse catch you unawares.

Why seek the wilderness?   Though there are no
   pathways,
beauty is no safer.   Hide in a wooded glade.
But when hot mid-day sun   stands huge and
   motionless,
water nymphs sundrily,   lustfully circle in,   780
grip handsome men tightly,   shameless in their spring
   flow.
Glade goddesses will slip   astride you lecherously
in your unguarded dreams.   Tree nymphs hunt every
   Pan
exploring mountain peaks.
                              The moon was born after
your chaste and pristine days   of old Arcadians.
As she looks down from skies   wild and starry above,
her power to steer a pure   and shining course will fail.
Not long ago she glowed   blush red though not a cloud
bridled with dirtied veil   her bright and willful face.

It sundered all our hearts   to see her power so
         bruised.   790
We clashed cymbals, rang bells,   we thought she was
   bewitched
by spells of Thessaly,   being forced down to earth.
But it was you. While she,   goddess of night, watched
   you,
she stopped in her swift course.   You held her back,
   and you
caused her suffering.

Cold's bite, we hope, will spare   the beauty of your face;
your looks should have but rare   exposure to the sun
so their sheen may be fair   as Parian marble.
How fine to see a face   fierce with virility
grim with old dignity   fashioned upon its brow!

Your radiant hair compares with Phoebus' untrimmed
  locks   800
which tumble shoulder-length, artlessly beautiful.
Yours lies lawless, brow-short, yet ruggedly handsome.
In fighting strength you'd dare challenge the roughest
  gods,
surpass them in the breadth of your great, spreading
  limbs.
Although you're young, you match the embedded
  muscles
of powerful Hercules. Your chest is broader than
that of the war god, Mars.
                              And if you wished to ride
upon a hard-hoofed mount, you could rein Cyllarus, 810
Castor's great Spartan horse, with a more agile hand.
With thumb and forefinger torque the javelin strap,
target the weapon, then hurl with your mighty strength.
Cretan hands, though well skilled with arrows and with
  bows,
shoot out their slender reeds a far shorter distance.
Or if fancy takes you to shoot in Parthian style,
spraying arrows skyward none will return to earth
without a bird transfixed, point plunged deep in its guts,
tumbling from veiling clouds.
                              Review the centuries:
rarely does beauty go unpunished among men.   820
May god treat you better! May he leave you safer,
and may he pass you by till your shapely beauty
crosses the threshold of age and shapelessness.
(*The* CHORUS *now either looks directly towards* PHAEDRA
and the NURSE, *if they are still on stage, or, if they have left,*
opens the palace door to give itself and the audience a glimpse
inside.)
What would a woman's passion fail to grasp
as she falls headlong down the precipice?
She plans to charge this innocent young man
with some atrocious crime. See, she parades
her schemes before our eyes.

                    The torn hair:
this is to be her proof. She ruffles up
her whole coiffure, dampens her cheeks with tears.
Every deceitful trick in woman's book
is used to further the illusion.

(*The* Nurse *leads* Phaedra *offstage if she still remains
there. She closes the palace doors behind them. Enter*
Theseus.)

But who is this approaching now? He seems
kingly in bearing and in countenance.   830
His face suggests he and Pirithous
would make a pair were it not for the cheeks:
how pale they are, how drained of all color!
Then there's the hair, all filthy and unkempt,
bristling on end. So Theseus himself
is here with us, back once again on earth.

ACT III

Theseus: I have at last crossed over the limits
of night's eternity, a refugee
from the vast dungeon of ghostly remains,
from dank blackness above me and around.
I yearned for daylight, yet my darkened eyes
can hardly bear it. For three years have passed,
four celebrations of the mysteries
at Eleusis, Triptolemus' harvests.
Four times has Libra's autumn equinox
balanced day against night. For all these months
I have endured a fate unknown before,
poised in the scales myself, hung up between
the pains of life and all the pains of death.   840
I was, in essence, dead. My sole remnant
of life was my ability to sense
and suffer pain.
                But then came Hercules:
ending infinity. He tore the dog
away from Tartarus and dragged it off.
He brought me back as well to where I stayed
during my life above.
                  But now my legs
are weak, my manliness tired and devoid
of its old, oaken firmness and resolve.
The struggle to get back from the deep pools
of Phlegethon up to the distant sky
was huge indeed. I was both fleeing death
and following the steps of Hercules.

The sound that drums my ears is of weeping.   850
What does this mean? Someone explain to me!

Grieving and tears and cries of suffering—
why these sad laments at my own door?
An apt homecoming, and auspicious too,
for someone who's returning from the dead!

(*Enter* NURSE *hurriedly from the palace. The* CHORUS *remains on stage during what follows. Since the* CHORUS *clearly suspects the* NURSE *is lying, some effort may be made to show its discomfort.*)

Nurse: Phaedra plans a killing, will not change
her resolve. We weep, but she spurns us
and is poised upon the brink of death.

Theseus: What makes her want to die? Her husband's back.

Nurse: Yet your return sharpens her wish to die.

Theseus: Your words are too involved. They cover up
something important. So speak openly,
tell me the anguish that afflicts her mind.

Nurse: She tells no one. She keeps her cause of grief
a secret. She's made up her mind to take   860
the pain that kills her to the grave. So come,
I beg you, come. We really must hurry.

Theseus: My royal home is locked. Open the doors!
(SERVANTS, *or possibly the* CHORUS, *open the palace doors, revealing* PHAEDRA *standing behind them.*)
You are the wife who shares my bed. You missed
your husband while he was away. Is this
how you should greet him when you see his face
on his return? Please give me heart to live,
widow your hand of its passion for steel.
What is it that drives you away from life?
won't you tell me?

Phaedra: Oh Lord! As you value
the symbols of your ruling power, Theseus,
man of noble heart, as you cherish
your children, now that you've returned, now I
am ashes on a pyre, please let me die. 870

Theseus: What makes you die, what cause compels your death?

Phaedra: If I tell you the cause, I waste my death.

Theseus: No ears but mine will hear what you shall say.

Phaedra: True wives fear only what their husbands hear.

Theseus: Speak. You can trust me, I'll keep it secret.

Phaedra: I know you'll hold your tongue if I hold mine.

Theseus: We won't leave you the means to kill yourself.

Phaedra: Death can't refuse you when you choose to die.

Theseus: What have you done that must be purged by death?

Phaedra: Remained alive.

Theseus: My tears—don't they move you? 880

Phaedra: To die and cause one's family to weep:
that is the finest way to leave this life.

Theseus: She still won't speak. We'll try fetters and whips
on the old nurse who will betray what she
refuses to admit. Clap her in chains:
The lash has power to extract secrets
from inside the mind.

Phaedra: Wait! I'll confess.

Theseus:	Why won't you look me in the eye, why are tears welling up? And tell me why you're trying to conceal them with your robe?
Phaedra:	Creator of what lies within the heavens, you are my witness, and so is the light which gleams in the bright sky, from which arose 890 my earthly family's origin. He begged, but I would not give in. He threatened me with steel. My courage held. But nonetheless, he had his violent wish. My blood will wash the ruin of my chastity away.
Theseus:	Out with it! Tell me who shamed my honor?
Phaedra:	Someone you'd least suspect.
Theseus:	Tell me his name.
Phaedra:	His sword will tell you. There was a lot of noise; My rapist feared people would come to help. He left it when he ran off terrified.
Theseus:	What kind of monstrous crime is this I see? Bright ivory on the hilt. And it's embossed with royal insignia in miniature— the famous crest of Athens. 900 He ran off. But where?
Phaedra	These servants saw him rush away, fast as he could, all upset and afraid.
Theseus:	O bonds of family love! O god who guides the stars, and Neptune, second-ranked, who stirs his realm with waves, whence comes this pestilence,

this offspring that I cannot bear to name?
Did Greek soil nurse him, or Bull Mountain Range,
Taurus, in Scythia, where Colchis lies
and where the Rioni flows? Bad blood reacts
recessively, reverts to primitive,
primordial, racial character.
                              His is
the madness of a race that fights like beasts,
loathes married sexuality, and keeps
the body pure for years but then makes it   910
common in vulgar promiscuity.
It is a filthy race that never yields
to any law that thrives in more moral
soil.
        Like beasts? But even beasts avoid
such sinful sexual acts. They all observe,
unconsciously, this natural taboo
in propagating their own race and kind.

So much for the stern look on that man's face,
all his fake loftiness, his homespun clothes,
his quest for old-time values, good old days,
his humorless, old-mannish, moral ways,
his shackled passions.
                          Your whole life's a lie!
You bury what you feel, you make your face
a pretty mask concealing your perverse
desires. Your modesty disguises your
immodesty; behind your passiveness
lurks prurience. Your pose as righteous son   920
hides all the filth of your unrighteousness.
Those who praise truth are frauds. Those who affect
rigid self-discipline are soft, debauched.

You woodsman, noble savage, pure and chaste,
were you saving your real self for me?

---

a race that fights like beasts: Amazons

Was it your pleasure, then, to show first proof
you were a man by the incestuous rape
of my wife in my bed?

                   I thank the heavens
I killed Antiope your own mother
with this very hand before I went
down to the caves of death. Better I did
than leave her here with you.

                    Be an outlaw,
on the run among peoples unknown
and distant. But you'll pay the penalty.
I don't care if you find the land beyond
the Ocean, at the limits of this world.   930
Settle in the Antipodes, bury
yourself deep within remotest caves
after crossing into realms of pack-ice
in the far north. And even if you get
beyond the winter cold, the white blizzards,
the howling, frigid threats of Arctic gales,
keep running, outlaw—I'll stay on your trail,
I'll find your lair. It may be far away,
closed off, concealed, or placed unreachably,
beyond the paths of men. But I'll get there,
for I can travel anyplace. You know   940
where I have just come from.

                 You may escape
to where weapons can't reach, but you will not
evade my curses. My father, the lord
of Ocean, gave me power to formulate
three wishes that the gods would have to grant.
He sealed his promise, swearing by the Styx.

Give me the grim gift you promised,
ruler of the sea!
Prevent Hippolytus from seeing
even one more dawn!
Young he is, but let him stay

among the ghostly dead
who still rage at me, his father.

You are my father:
help me do the task I wish that
I could will away.
I would never use this last gift
of your godly power
were it not that dreadful evils
press upon me hard.   950
When I saw the pit of darkness
and Death's hideous face,
the real meaning of the menace
in Pluto's dead realm,
I refrained still from my third wish.

But now it is time.
You swore me an oath. Stand by it.
Why do you delay?
Father, why are your waves silent?
Let the winds arise,
drive dark clouds to veil the night sky,
snatch the stars away,
pour your seas forth, bring the forces
of the common sea,
and call on the swollen hugeness
of Ocean itself.

Chorus: Birth force, the mighty   parent of gods' power,
and you, the lord of   Olympus' lightning,   960
who fling scattered stars   in spatial fastness,
hurl vagrant planets   in wandering orbits,
make the night sky spin   swift on its axis,
tell me what makes   you meticulously
maintain exact paths   in heaven, forever?
Your work ensures that   sharp bite of hoarfrost
will strip the forests,   that spring will bring back

shade beneath tree limbs,   that summer's lion
will roast to ripeness   cereal harvests,
and that the year's flow   will regulate the   970
force of his fierceness.

God, you control such   hugeness of movement,
you keep in balance   the immense weight of
all the vast cosmos   in its revolutions.
Are you the same god   who is so removed from
human existence?   You are so distant,
and never stir to   help good men or harm
those who are evil.

Luck is the demon   who rules our human
lives with her chaos.   She deals her scattered
gifts from a blind hand,   favors the evil.   980
Sickening lust makes   saints succumb to her,
fraud rules as despot   in halls of power,
the people find joy   in giving high office
to a vile man. They   adore those they hate most.
Manliness grows grim   as it endures the
perverse fruits of justice.   Poverty follows
hard on clean living,   but vice is potent:
adultery's king.

An empty word, shame. Honor? a cheap trick.

A messenger hurries towards us now.
His face expresses sorrow, and his cheeks
are wet with tears. I wonder what this means.   990

---

summer's lion: The sun is in the sign of Leo during mid-summer

ACT IV

Enter MESSENGER.

Messenger: Fate is both hard and bitter, slavery
itself a heavy weight. So why does chance
select me as its messenger of doom?

Theseus: Courage! Don't be afraid of me. State
your catastrophe. My heart is steeled
for sorrow's ravages. I am prepared.

Messenger: My tongue will not express the pain I feel
and which, if voiced, will bring its hearers grief.

Theseus: This house is shattered now. You may proclaim
whatever fate adds on to weigh it down.

Messenger: Hippolytus, god help me, has been killed.
He died a wretched, pitiable death.

Theseus: My son died quite a while ago, as I,
his father, know. What you report now is
some rapist's death. So tell the whole story.

Messenger: Anger was in his step when he left town,   1000
a fugitive, threading his way swiftly
through the maze of streets with hurried stride.
A bit too hastily he slipped the yoke
upon his thoroughbreds, bridled their heads,
threaded the reins in tight. He talked a lot,
and to himself. He wished that he could will
his father's land away with oaths. He called

90

his father's name out loudly several times.
He let the reins go slack and then sharply
flicked them like a whip. At this moment,
the vast sea thundered with a sudden roar,
rising from its depths, crescendoing
up to the stars. No wind turned brine to spray,
no dark stormheads crackled above. The sky
was clear. The tempest roughening the waves
was the sea's own product, more violent   1010
than southerlies churning Messina's straits,
than the Ionian Sea, its bosom mad
with passion and swelling beneath north winds,
as cliffs shudder with ferocious surf
and white spray pounds on Leucate's white cape.
The huge sea surges up erect, into
a vast, destructive mound. The deep, swollen
with the beast inside, rushes to land.
This crushing force was not built to assail
shipping, but to terrify the land.
The surf curls forward, swift and violent;
the water carries in its curving womb
something—I don't know what. Is earth perhaps
extending some new pinnacle towards   1020
the stars, is a new island rising in
the Cyclades? You can no longer see
the cliffs of Epidauros' healing god,
the Rocks of Sciron, famous for their crimes,
the Isthmus—land squeezed in between two seas.
While we are in a stupor, puzzling
this out, the whole sea bellows, every cliff
echoes the sound, the tallest promontory
is left dew-damp with spurted salt sea-spray,
alternately foaming, washed with waves,
then spewing water back.
                              Compare a whale
swimming on high seas between Ocean's shores.
He sucks in vast quantities of brine,
then spouts them from his breathing hole in waves. 1030

91

This massive bubble of water shuddered
and burst, exploding outwards, sweeping
to shore a beast, evil beyond our fears.
The sea roared onto land in full pursuit
of its monster.

               My lips quiver with fear.
How to describe the way that vast thing looked!
Its body was a bull's, extremely tall,
its neck a dark blue color, its forehead
greenish; on it, erect, a lengthy mane.
The ears were shaggy and pricked up; the eyes,
varied in color and suggesting both
the dominating bull of a wild herd
and something native to the sea. See them
from one perspective and those eyes spew flames,   1040
from yet another they are glittering
with light refracted in marine dark blue.
The splendid neck flexes bulging muscles,
the nostrils open cavernously wide
and snort as they inhale. Dewlap and chest
are green with algae, long extended flanks
reddened with kelp. And at the hindquarters
its shape merges into monstrosity:
a huge and scaly creature dragging its
infinity of length, making one think
of the leviathans in mid-ocean
that gulp ships down or shatter them.

                      The earth
trembled, cattle fled wildly across
the farmlands as they do in thunderstorms.   1050
The thought of chasing his prize bullocks down
escapes the drover. All the wild game flees
its secret woodland pastures. Yet hunters
stand prickling with horror, drained of blood,
chilled with a fear only Hippolytus
fights off. Reins tight, he holds the horses in.

They are frightened, yet they still know the voice
he uses coaxingly to urge them on.

A path leads over broken hills to farms,
hugging the coastline high above the sea.
Here the massive creature works itself
to rage, honing itself to readiness.
Its courage fired, its rage sufficiently
rehearsed, it flies on down at breakneck speed,   1060
its feet moving so fast they scarcely skim
the surface of the ground.
                        And then it stopped.
It faced the quivering team with bullying
arrogance. Your son arose to meet
this bestial challenge with threats in his eyes.
There was no change in either voice or face.
He thundered out: "You're wasting time trying
to frighten me. You can't break my spirit.
My father's special work was fighting bulls."
Right then his horses broke from his control.
Bolting they tore his chariot from the path,
lunging any way the violence
of fear conveyed them in their mad panic,   1070
driving themselves among the great boulders.

When stormy seas run high, a skipper keeps
his vessel under some control, prevents
it swinging broadside to the swell, and foils
the waves with all his practised skill. Likewise
Hippolytus still guided his coursers.
Using the reins, he keeps the pressure on,
limits the movement of their heads. His wrist
constantly snaps the whip upon their backs.
But his companion sticks unshakably
with him. One moment it runs side by side,
matching the horses in their stride; the next
it circles round to face and head them off,
shifting the terror, leaving no escape.

There was no longer any place to run.   1080
The hideous horned creature from the sea
confronted them head–on. Their minds were spurred
by fear of what they saw, their pounding feet
tore free of all command, they fought to break
from harness. Rearing up on their hind legs
they tossed their burden off. He was spilled out
head first, facedown. And as he fell the reins
looped round his body, gripped it like a noose.
The more he struggled, the tighter he drew
the knots. The animals themselves were trained
to human hands and sensed they had done wrong:
the chariot was light, no one now held
control. They rushed about at fear's command.

One thinks about the solar chariot team
which sensed a different weight upon its wheels,
and felt slighted that daylight was assigned   1090
to a false Sun. So, wandering from its course,
it shook Phaethon out.
                              His blood spatters
tilled fields, his head smashes against boulders,
whiplashes back. Briars rip out his hair,
sharp gravel scars, dehumanizes his
attractive face; his beauty vanishes
in multiplicity of wounds. His limbs
are dying, but the chariot wheels roll on.
Then finally, as he is still ravaged,
a tree-trunk, charred into a stump, pointed
and erect, pins him through the groin,
transfixing him. Its master's impalement,
just for an instant, stops the chariot   1100
until the harnessed pair breaks the delay
and, at the same time, breaks its master too.
He is still half alive. Virgin bushland,
brambles toughly armed with sharpened thorns,
slice into him. Each tree trunk owns some part
of his body.

Now they are wandering,
his handful of attendants, through the fields,
upon an errand of sorrow and death.
They search the places where Hippolytus,
as he was torn apart, left a long trail
marked with blood. His keening dogs now track
their master's limbs. But careful scrutiny
by those who grieve has been unable yet
to yield a whole body.

(SERVANTS *bring in a stretcher on which lie* HIPPOLYTUS'
bloodied remains.)

Beauty of form:
is it reduced to this?   1110

Moments ago,
he shared empire in glorious partnership
with his father, he was the obvious heir.
Like a star, he blazed. Now particles
of him are picked up as they're found and brought
for funeral rituals and cremation fires.

(THESEUS *goes over to the bier.*)

Theseus: Nature, the power of kinship is too great.
You shackle parents with a bond of blood.
Though, for the life of me, I do not want
to reverence you, I do.

                                        He did me wrong.
I wanted to destroy him. Nonetheless,
now he is lost to me, I am in tears.

Messenger: You wanted this to happen, so you have
no honest pretext for the tears you weep.

Theseus: It is the pinnacle of sorrow when
chance makes us wish that we could will away
the very things we so desired to see.   1120

Messenger: If you still hate him, why are you weeping?

95

Theseus: I weep because I killed him, not because
              I lost either my anger or my son.

              (THESEUS *collapses sobbing. The* CHORUS *circles round him
              and addresses the audience.*)

Chorus: Fortune's great downdrafts   whirl the fates of humans
              but her rage steals less   violently on small folk.
              God's steel fist falls   less weighty on the weightless;
              their faceless silence   keeps them safely tranquil,
              their paltry huts—   safekeeping until old age.

              Mountain peaks surge up,   threaten sky's sure havens
              and catch the east winds   as they catch the south winds
              and manic northers' menace,   1130
              and nor'westers' rainsqualling.
              Valleys, though rain-damp,   rarely suffer bolts from
              ominous lightning.
              Towering Caucasus   and tall woods of Ida,
              home of Cybele,   shiver at high-pealing
              Jupiter's thunder.   For he fears and targets
              things close to heaven,   like kings in their castles.
              Earth-hugging homes of   common men are never
              struck by his blasting.   1140

              Forward flies time with   up and down wingstrokes;
              fortune is fleet so   she will stand by no one,
              faithless as ever.
              This man emerged from   night into bright starlight,
              then into sunshine   yet found no delight in
              his grim return to   homecoming more mournful
              than death's Avernus.

              Pallas, still virgin,   adored by the Athenians,
              you owe no debt to   Pluto, your rapist uncle.
              True, your own Theseus   sees the sky, the living,   1150
              and he escaped from   Styx's deathly waters.

But Pluto has the   same number of corpses.

(PHAEDRA *screams from inside the palace.*)

I hear a pealing cry of mourning deep
within the high castle. And now I see
Phaedra, sword drawn, grief-mad. What will she do?

ACT V

Enter PHAEDRA.

Theseus: What passion lashes you with pain like this?
            Why are you armed? What are your screams and moans
            over this corpse we hate meant to express?

Phaedra: I am the one that you should surge upon,
            wild power that dominates the bounded sea's
            unbounded depths! Send dark blue Ocean's beasts
            out after me! Inside her inmost womb   1160
            the sea herself must nurture some monster,
            and Ocean must conceal within himself
            some creature in his fluctuating tides
            by distant shores!
                            Theseus, what a harsh man
            you always are! Your family's never safe
            when you come back. Your father and your son
            have paid the price of death for your return.
            Perverse destroyer of your home, you kill,
            whether you love or hate your current wife.

            Hippolytus, did I do this to you,
            and turn your face into what I now see?
            What savage beast, the kind your father kills,
            dismembered you? Perhaps some new Sinis,
            or a Procrustes, or a Minotaur
            from Crete that fills with bellowing its maze   1170
            made by another Daedalus ripped you
            ferociously with horns upon its head.

Your father: Aegeus

98

Where has your beauty gone, where are those eyes,
my stars of heaven? All lost.
                              You can't be dead!
Come back for just a moment! Listen to
my words, there's nothing shameful in them now.
With my own hand I penalize myself
for what I did to you, and I will thrust
this blade of steel into my sinful heart.
In doing so I purge Phaedra of crime
as well as life. Then I will follow you
across the waters, Tartarus' lakes,
across the Styx, master the streams of fire,   1180
maddened with love.
                              Let me now satisfy
your ghost.
                      Here, guard this lock, this hair lopped from
my forehead where I cut the scalp. In life
we could not be a couple, but in death
it is allowed.
                      Now die.
                              If you are chaste,
die for your husband; if incestuous,
die for your love.
                      I cannot go into
our room again; our marriage is too stained
with crime, and it would be the final sin
to take my pleasure in that bed once more,
as if I were the loyal wife avenged.
Death, you relieve the evil of my love;
death, you are the decent path from shame.
I run to you. Open your arms. Forgive.   1190

Athens, listen to me. You too, Theseus:
I am a stepmother, and I bring death,
but you, a father, are much worse than I.
What I told you was false, the rape a lie
which I invented, drunk with fantasy,
heartsick with love. And you punished a crime

that never was, fine father. This young man
was chaste and virginally innocent,
killed by the accusation of incest.
Your honor is restored. My sinful breast
provides a path for justice and the sword;
my blood is ritual appeasement for
the spirit of this pure and holy man.

You, his parent. Let his stepmother
teach you your duty, now your son is gone.
Plunge yourself into the lakes of Hell.   1200

(PHAEDRA *stabs herself with* HIPPOLYTUS' *sword*.)

Theseus: Jaws of skeletal Avernus,
cavern of Taenarum,
waters of Lethe, joy to the suffering,
lakes of stillness!
Hide this sinful father,
drown him,
crush him in the bite of
eternal evil.

Fierce deep creatures,
vast devastating sea,
upon me now
with whatever horror Proteus conceals
in sea's inmost recess.
I triumphed in monstrous crime,
so tear me away,
into your maelstrom throats!

Father, always ready to approve
and to fulfill my anger,
I tore my son to pieces,
strewed him across fields—
a novel form of death, devised for him.
I do not deserve an easy death myself.
While I played executioner,

sternly avenging
an outrage that never was,
I fell into a hideous act of crime.   1210
Now I have filled the skies,
the world of death,
the seas, with my atrocities.
The three realms know me now;
there is no further place that I can go.

Did I come back for this? The farthest path
to the celestial world just opened up
so there could be revealed two funerals,
a double death to see, so celibate
and sonless I could sear with just one torch
the future of my house, my hopes of love?

Hercules, how dark the light you gave!
I was your gift from Death. Now send me back.
Return me to the ghosts you snatched me from.

I left Death behind. Now, when I've sinned,
I beg in vain to die.
                    You are no more
than a crude architect of death who plans   1220
unusual and cruel ends. Sentence
yourself now to your just punishment.
Have them bend a pine until its top
touches the ground. Then let it be released,
rending you in two.
                    Should they hurl me
from the precipitous Scironian cliffs?
I have seen worse—the pains that Phlegethon
forces the guilty to endure: the grief
of fire encasing you in endless stream.
I do not speculate about the pain
or place which will await my soul. I know.

I have filled the skies: Ariadne, betrayed by Theseus, became a star

Guilty ghosts, make space for me. My neck
must bear the heavy burden and my hands
weary the stone. For Sisyphus grows old   1230
in his eternal toil. I am the one
whose lips the lapping water surely should
now tantalize. The ruthless vulture must
leave Tityus and fly over to me,
bringing eternal, penal suffering
as my liver regrows. And Ixion,
father of Pirithous, my friend,
relax. The wheel torqued up to whirlwind speed
can turn my limbs in ever-spinning course.
Earth, open up your jaws, and take me back
into that hideous chasm. For this is
a juster way for me to join the ghosts.
I follow my son.
          King of the dead,
no need to be afraid. I do not come
to carry off your wife. Please take me back   1240
in your eternal home. I will not leave
again.
         My prayers have failed to move the gods.
If I asked evil, they would trip in haste.

Chorus: Eternity remains for your complaints.
This, Theseus, is the time to pay the dues
you owe your son: a speedy burial
for his scattered parts that were torn up
so bestially and so disgracefully.

Theseus: Bring to me what is left of his body.
and heap his limbs together randomly.
Oh how I cared for him!
               Hippolytus,
it is my crime, not you I recognize.
I murdered you. I am accountable
not just on this one charge, nor did I act
alone. When I, your parent, dared to plan   1250

this deed, I asked my father for his help.
I thus enjoy my father's offering.
A grim fate for an old and broken man,
to be left childless.
                              Then embrace his limbs,
your son's relics, you pitiable fool.
Prostrate yourself, clasp them to your sad heart.

Chorus: You created him. Reset the limbs
of this torn body back in proper place,
restore him from the parts that fled away.
His brave right hand goes here. The left, with which
he held the reins so skillfully, goes here.
I see traces of his torso's left side.   1260

So much is missing, absent from my grief.

Theseus: My hands, as they perform their ghoulish task,
are trembling. Be steady! Don't convulse
with sobs and tears, my cheeks, stay dry until
the father who created him re-forms
his son's body, accounts for all his limbs.
This piece is formless and grotesque, sundered
from every side with wounds. I cannot tell
what part of you it is, but it is part.
So set it in an empty place—in here.
Is this the shining face, bright, like a star,
with fire, that forced his enemies to turn
their eyes away? His beauty changed to this?   1270
How grim fate is, how bestial the goodwill
of godly power! A parent prayed his son
would return home like this. The prayer: granted.

Take, then, these final offerings that I,
your father and creator, give to you.
So many fragments, many funerals!
Let fire cremate, meanwhile, what we have here.

Open my house, so bitter to me now
with death and slaughter. Let Mopsopia,
all Athens, ring with peals of wild lament.
Kindle the flames, men, for a royal pyre.
The rest of you, hunt through the fields to see
if some parts of the corpse eluded you.

And her? Dig out a trench. Pile earth on top.
Lay heavy soil on her ungodly head.   1280

Glossary

The brief summaries given here are based on the Senecan versions of the myths. Other ancient writers often give different accounts. Variants are mentioned only where necessary for clarity. An asterisk next to a name indicates that it has its own entry elsewhere in the glossary. The Latin names are used except when an accepted English version exists.

Absyrtus   Son of Aeetes* and brother of Medea;* killed by Medea, who then threw his limbs into the sea as she fled from Colchis.*

Acastus   King of Iolcus,* in Thessaly;* son of Pelias,* Jason's* uncle and enemy.

Achaean   Greek.

Acharnia   An area in Attica* north of Athens.

Acheron   One of four frequently mentioned rivers of the Greek underworld.

Achilles   Son of the goddess Thetis* and her mortal husband, Peleus,* born in Phthia* in Thessaly;* educated by the centaur Chiron.* At the outbreak of the Trojan War, Thetis disguised him as a girl (to keep him from being drafted into the army) and kept him on the island of Scyros,* where he raped a girl named Deidamia, thus fathering Pyrrhus.* Eventually he betrayed himself to the Greek military recruiters, led by Ulysses,* by his fascination with the weapons they brought.

Acte   Another name for Attica.*

Admetus   Mythical king of Thessaly* whose wife, Alcestis,* died in his place but was brought back from the dead by Hercules.*

Aeacus   Father of Peleus;* grandfather of Achilles;* frequently thought of as a ruler among the dead.

Aeetes   King of Colchis;* father of Medea* and Absyrtus.*

Aegaleus   A mountain range in Attica.*

Aegeus   Father of Theseus.★ The Aegean Sea was named for him. See Sunion.

Aeolus   Father of Sisyphus;★ ancestor of Creon★ of Corinth★ and his daughter Creusa.★

Aeson   Father of Jason;★ king of Iolcus,★ deposed by Pelias.★

Aetna   A volcano in Sicily; mythical abode of Vulcan,★ god of fire.

Agamemnon   King of Mycenae;★ son of Atreus,★ brother of Menelaus.★ Leader of the Greek expedition against Troy,★ he sacrificed his own daughter to obtain favorable winds (see Aulis). His quarrel with Achilles,★ who objected to Agamemnon's seizure of his concubine Briseis,★ is a major motif of Homer's *Iliad*.

Ajax   (1) The "Greater" Ajax, son of Telamon, was the best of the Greek warriors at Troy★ after Achilles;★ he committed suicide when the dead Achilles' armor was awarded to Ulysses★ rather than to him. (2) The "Lesser" Ajax, son of Oileus,★ was shipwrecked on his return from the Trojan War.

Alcestis   Wife of Admetus.★ She was brought back to life by Hercules★ after she died in her husband's place.

Alcides   A descendant of Alc(a)eus, the father of Amphitryon; always = Hercules★ in Seneca.

Alcmena   Wife of Amphitryon. Seduced by Jupiter,★ who disguised himself as her husband, she gave birth to Hercules.★

Alpheus   A river in the Peloponnesus.

Althaea   Mother of Meleager,★ whose life, she was told at his birth, could last only as long as a certain log burning in the fire. She immediately seized the log from the flames, but years later, when Meleager killed her beloved brothers, in anger she threw it back into a fire. As predicted, Meleager died when the log was consumed.

Amazons   A group of nomadic, man-hating female warriors whose homeland is usually given as the region around the Black Sea: Maeotis,★ Thermodon,★ Pontus.★ The Greeks had several mythical battles with them. Theseus★ fought them and forced Antiope★ to become his wife; she bore him a son, Hippolytus,★ but Theseus later put her to death. Penthesilea★ led a band of Amazons against the Greeks at Troy and was killed by Achilles.★

Amor   Cupid;★ especially popular among the Roman poets because his name spelled backward is Roma. In Vergil's *Aeneid* and elsewhere in Latin literature, Aeneas, founder of the Roman race, is Amor's brother.

Amyclae   A city near Sparta;★ Sparta's "twin city." Its name is often used to indicate Sparta itself.

Ancaeus   An Argonaut from Tegea, in the Peloponnesus, who replaced Tiphys★ as helmsman of the *Argo*★ after Tiphys' death.

Andromache   Daughter of Eetion;★ wife of Hector;★ mother of Astyanax.★

She was taken from Troy★ by Pyrrhus★ after the city's fall and was ultimately married to Hector's brother, Helenus.★

Antenor   A Trojan warrior; husband of Theano, priestess of the goddess Minerva (Pallas)★ at Troy.★ In some traditions Antenor and Aeneas, son of Venus,★ betrayed Troy to the Greeks.

Antiope   A queen of the Amazons.★ She appears in three distinct traditions: (1) as a wife of Theseus★ (see Amazons); (2) as the queen whose girdle Hercules★ must win as his ninth labor; (3) as mother of Amphion and Zethus, the builders of Thebes'★ walls.

Aonia   Thebes.★

Aphidnae   An area of Attica★ near Marathon.★

Apollo   See Phoebus.

Aquilo   See Boreas.

Araxes   An Armenian river, today the Aras; often a symbol to Roman writers of the eastern boundary of Roman power.

Arcadia   A mountainous and primitive part of Greece whose inhabitants were supposedly the earliest inhabitants of Greece; they are often depicted as people of either ideal simplicity or primitive barbarism. Roman tradition maintained that the first settlement of the site of Rome was made by an exiled king of Arcadia, Evander, a descendant of Lycaon,★ "Wolfman."

Arctus   The constellation Ursa Major (the Great Bear or Big Dipper), the main constellation used by the Greeks for navigation. The Phoenicians and Carthaginians sailed by the Lesser Bear (Ursa Minor), known as Cynosura. In myth the Great Bear is Callisto,★ daughter of Lycaon.★ After her rape by Jupiter★ she was turned into a bear by Diana,★ then saved from hunters by Jupiter,★ who placed her in the skies.

Argo   The ship that conveyed Jason★ and the Argonauts (i.e., "sailors in *Argo*") to and from Colchis;★ in some traditions, the first ship ever made. *Argo*'s keel was made of oak from the prophetic shrine of Dodona; the vessel itself could speak.

Argos   A major city in the Peloponnesus, often not distinguished from Mycenae.★ The adjective "Argive" is often used to mean "Greek."

Ariadne   Daughter of Minos,★ king of Crete, and of Pasiphae,★ his wife; sister of Phaedra★ and the Minotaur.★ She fell in love with Theseus★ and saved him from death in the labyrinth by supplying him with a thread made by Daedalus★ which enabled Theseus to escape from the labyrinth after killing the Minotaur, who was imprisoned there. Theseus took Ariadne with him as he left Crete but abandoned her on the island of Naxos. She was saved by Bacchus,★ who made her his wife and ultimately set her in the heavens as a star.

Assaracus   Great-grandson of Dardanus;★ brother of Jupiter's★ Trojan lover Ganymede; great-grandfather of Aeneas, who was regarded by some Roman writers as founder of the Roman people.

Assyria Very roughly the equivalent of parts of modern Iraq; to Roman writers it included Syria as well. The area was proverbial for its luxurious living and particularly for its perfumes.

Astyanax Son of Hector* and Andromache;* killed on instructions from Calchas.*

Athos A high peninsula jutting out into the Aegean from the Thracian coast.

Atreus Father of Agamemnon* and Menelaus* (who are collectively known as the Atridae); feuded with his brother Thyestes,* whose children he murdered and served as a meal to their father.

Attica The section of Greece in which the city of Athens is situated.

Aulis A coastal city of Euboea, in Greece, from which the Greeks sailed to Troy.* Here, to obtain favorable winds, Agamemnon* sacrificed his daughter Iphigenia at the bidding of the priest Calchas.*

Ausonian A general poetic term for the non-Greek-speaking ancient inhabitants of Italy.

Auster The south wind, bringer of clouds and rain.

Avernus The Italian equivalent of Taenarum;* a lake near Cumae, in the Bay of Naples area, which supposedly welled up from the underworld.

Bacchus God of wine, proverbially beautiful; also known as Lyaeus, Liber, Bromius, and Dionysus.

Baetis The river Guadalquivir, in Spain.

Bessa A small town near Scarphe,* in Locris (central Greece).

Boötes A constellation near the Greater and Lesser Bears.

Boreas The north wind, father of Calais* and Zetes.*

Briseis A woman from Lyrnesos* captured by Achilles* and kept as his lover. She was seized from Achilles by Agamemnon* when Agamemnon was forced to relinquish his own captive lover, Chryseis.*

Bromius See Bacchus.

Busiris A mythical Egyptian king who sacrificed at the altar of Jupiter* all foreigners who entered his land.

Calais Son of Boreas;* twin of Zetes; drove off the Harpies* from their homeland; killed (with Zetes) by Hercules.*

Calchas A Greek prophet who told Agamemnon* he must sacrifice his own daughter to obtain favorable winds for the voyage to Troy.* He also ordered that Astyanax* and Polyxena* be sacrificed to secure the Greeks' safe return.

Callisto Daughter of Lycaon.* See Arctus.

Calydnae Two small islands off the coast of Asia Minor, near Troy.*

Calydon Town in Aetolia (Greece), most famous in myth for a boar hunt which took place there. It was during this hunt that Meleager* killed his uncles.

Camena The Latin equivalent of the Greek *Mousa*, Muse. Seneca's choice of this word to indicate the mother of the Greek bard Orpheus★ is striking, as Roman poets tended to use *Musa* rather than *Camena* in reference to Greek poetic muses. Compare his use of the Latin term *fescennine*.★

Carystos   A city at the south end of the island of Euboea (Greece).

Cassandra   Daughter of Priam★ and Hecuba;★ priestess of Phoebus.★ She agreed to become the god's lover in return for the gift of prophecy but finally refused to have sex with him. Phoebus punished her by decreeing that no one would believe her prophecies. After the fall of Troy★ she was assigned to Agamemnon★ as his prize.

Castor   Brother of Pollux;★ one of *Argo*'s crew. The two brothers, who spent half of each year alive and half dead, were known and worshiped together as the divine Dioscuri ("Boys of Zeus," in Greek) and were believed to protect sailors. Castor was famous for his horsemansip and his horse Cyllarus; Pollux was famous for his boxing.

Caucasus   A mountain or mountainous area near the Caspian Sea; the mythical site where Prometheus★ was kept in chains.

Caycus   The principal river of Mysia★ (Turkey).

Cecrops   A mythical forebear of the Athenian people, half man, half snake. The adjective "Cecropian" is often used as a general equivalent of "Athenian."

Cephallenia   An Ionian★ island southwest of Ithaca; the name is often used to indicate Ithaca.

Cerberus   A mythical three-headed dog who guarded the entrance/exit of the underworld.

Ceres   Mother Earth; goddess of crops.

Chalcis   A powerful city of Euboea (Greece), one of whose colonies was Cumae, in Italy.

Charybdis   A dangerous mythical whirlpool in the sea, facing Scylla.★

Chimaera   A mythical monster, part goat, part lion, part snake.

Chiron   A centaur (half horse, half man) associated with Mount Pelion,★ in Thessaly;★ tutor of Achilles.★ Although immortal, he was wounded by Hercules★ with a poisoned arrow, and in his pain begged to be allowed to die.

Chryse   A small town near Troy.★

Chryseis   Daughter of Chryses, a priest of Phoebus;★ taken as a concubine by Agamemnon★ but released when Phoebus sent a plague upon the Greek army. Agamemnon took Briseis★ from Achilles★ as a replacement for Chryseis.

Cicero   A Roman orator of the first century B.C. In his first oration against Catiline (a Roman noble who Cicero believed was plotting to overthrow the government), Cicero appealed to Catiline to "free the citizens from fear" by leaving Rome. Seneca's Creon★ echoes these words in *Medea*.

Cilla   A small town near Chryse.★

Cnossos   The principal city of ancient Crete; home of Minos,★ Phaedra,★ and the Minotaur.

Colchis   Medea's★ hometown, on the eastern shore of the Black Sea (now in the Soviet Union).

Corinth   A city on the isthmus connecting the Peloponnesus to northern Greece.

Corus   The northwest wind.

Cossack   = Scythian★ in these translations.

Creon   King of Corinth;★ father of Creusa.★

Creusa   Daughter of Creon.★

Cupid   God of love = Amor,★ often represented by Romans as the son of Venus.★

Cybele   The earth-mother goddess (also known as Cybebe), whose cult was centered on Mount Ida,★ near Troy,★ Her cult was also well established in Rome.

Cyclades   Islands in the Aegean.

Cygnus   The invulnerable son of Neptune,★ whom Achilles★ killed by strangulation; Neptune metamorphosed him into a swan.

Cyllarus   The special horse of Castor.★

Daedalus   An Athenian craftsman, who helped the Cretan queen Pasiphae★ consummate her love for a white bull by making her a cowsuit of wood. Pasiphae's child by this mating, the Minotaur, was imprisoned within a maze (labyrinth) designed by Daedalus at the request of Pasiphae's husband, Minos.★ After Daedalus helped the lovesick Ariadne★ save Theseus★ from death in the labyrinth—he gave her a ball of thread that enabled Theseus to retrace his steps—Minos imprisoned him (in, according to some accounts, his own artistic marvel, the labyrinth). Daedalus escaped with his son, Icarus, by creating wings of feathers and wax, but Icarus fell to earth and died because he flew too close to the sun, which melted the wax of his wings.

Danaans   The people of Danaus★ (king of Argos★); the Greeks.

Danaids   The fifty daughters of Danaus,★ king of Argos,★ who, with one exception, killed their husbands, the sons of Aegyptus, king of Egypt.

Danaus   King of Argos.★

Dardanus   Ancestor of the people of Troy;★ son of Teucer★ or of Jupiter.★ In some traditions, Dardanus arrived in Troy from Italy.

Deucalion   The Greek Noah; one of two survivors of the Great Flood sent by Jupiter★ to punish sinful mortals. See Pyrrha.

Diana   Sister of Phoebus,★ also called Phoebe;★ goddess of the moon and of magic; often indistinguishable from Hecate.★

Dictynna   A Cretan goddess, identified with Diana.★

Diomedes   (1) A companion of Ulysses.★ In a famous night expedition at Troy,★ the two killed a Trojan spy, Dolon, and a newly arrived Trojan ally, Rhesus,★ and his men. They then made off with Rhesus' wonderful horses. (2) A mythical king of Thrace★ who fed human flesh to his horses until Hercules★ took the horses away from him.

Dis   God of (buried) wealth; god of the dead = Pluto.★

dryads   Female tree spirits (nymphs) often pursued by (or in pursuit of) the god Pan.★

Eetion   Father of Andromache;★ killed, along with his seven sons, by Achilles.★

Eleusis   A city in Attica,★ famous as the site of the rites of the goddess Ceres★ (Greek Demeter).

Elysium   The (underworld) home of the blessed dead.

Endymion   A handsome youth with whom the Moon (Diana)★ fell in love, and who, in many versions of the myth, sleeps eternally.

Enispe   A small town in Arcadia★ (Greece).

Epidauros   A coastal town not far from Argos★ (Greece), famous for its temple of Aesculapius, the god of healing and medicine.

Erebus   The darkness of death and the underworld; the underworld itself.

Erinys   The goddess of vendettas, who avenges bloodguilt; often named either Megaera★ or Tisiphone.

Eryx   Son of Venus★ and Hercules,★ in whose honor a mountain in Sicily (famous for its temple of Venus) was named.

Europa   Daughter of Agenor, a king of Phoenicia (ancient Lebanon); sister of Cadmus, founder of Thebes★ (Greece); abducted by Jupiter★ disguised as a bull; mother of Minos,★ king of Crete.

Fate   That which is spoken or decreed; destiny, fate.

Fescennine   A ribald, farcical Italian song, sung at Roman weddings; one of the specifically Italian elements in Seneca's representation of Jason's★ wedding. See Camena.

Fortune   An Italian goddess, (temperamental) bringer of produce and good luck.

Furies   Vengeful spirits of the dead. See Erinys.

Gaetulians   People of North Africa (Tunis and Morocco).

Garamantians   People of Saharan Africa.

Getae   Nomadic and barbaric Thracian (Balkan) people.

Gonoessa   A small town near Sicyon, in the Peloponnesus (Greece).

Gradivus   The stepping, marching god: Mars.★

Greater Bear   See Arctus.

Gyrton   Town in Thessaly★ (Greece).

Haemus   A great Balkan mountain range.

Harpies   Monstrous creatures, part bird, part woman, chased from their home by the twin sons of Boreas.★ See Calais;★ Zetes.

Hebrus   A Thracian river (modern Maritza) which flows into the Aegean.

Hecate   Goddess of moon, magic, and witchcraft, also of crossroads; often called Trivia, "three-way path." See Diana.

Hector   Chief Trojan warrior in the war at Troy;★ son of Priam;★ husband of Andromache;★ killed by Achilles.★ Hector's body was ransomed from the Greeks by Priam.

Hecuba   Wife of Priam;★ mother of Hector,★ Cassandra,★ Polyxena,★ Paris,★ and Helenus.★

Helen   Daughter of Jupiter★ (or Tyndareus)★ and Leda; wife of Menelaus,★ king of Sparta;★ awarded by Venus★ as a prize to Paris★ (son of Priam,★ who took her away to Troy★ (see Ida). Her abduction triggered the Trojan War. After Paris' death she was married to his brother Deiphobus.

Helenus   Twin brother of Cassandra★ and, like her, a prophet; one of the few male survivors of Trojan royal blood; subsequently became king of Buthrotum, in Epirus.

Helle   Daughter of Athamas and Nephele. Her mother saved her from being sacrificed and sent her and her brother Phrixus★ out to sea on the back of a sheep with a fleece of gold. Helle drowned in the Hellespont (named for her), but Phrixus traveled on to Colchis,★ where the sheep was sacrificed and became the Golden Fleece, the object of Jason's★ and the Argonauts' quest.

Hercules   Son of Jupiter★ and Alcmena.★ He sailed on the *Argo*★ but was left behind when his friend Hylas★ failed to return to the ship and Hercules stayed ashore too long searching for him. He was the strongest of Greek heroes; his bow, inherited by Philoctetes, was supposedly the critical weapon in the final struggle for Troy.★ Among his other labors, he killed the many-headed water snake, the Hydra,★ whose poison Medea★ wanted. His prowess at killing snakes first manifested itself when, as a child still in his cradle, he strangled two snakes that Juno★ had sent to kill him. Yet this masculine hero dressed as a maid when in love with Omphale.

Hercynian Forest   A vast forestland in ancient central Europe.

Hermione   Daughter of Helen★ and Menelaus;★ married to Pyrrhus,★ who was murdered by Orestes;★ finally married Orestes.

Hesperus   The evening star; the west.

Hippolytus   Son of Theseus★ and the Amazon★ Antiope.★

Hister   The river Danube.

Hyades   (1) Daughters of Atlas. (2) The Zodiacal constellation Hyades ("Rainers").

Hydaspes   A tributary of the Indus River.

Hydra   A many-headed snake killed by Hercules★ at Lerna.★

Hylas   See Hercules.

Hymen   (1) God of (marriage) feasts. (2) A song (hymn) sung at weddings.

Hymettus   The most southerly of the three major mountains in Attica,★ famous for its honey.

Hyrcanians   People who lived near the Caspian Sea.

Ida   A well-timbered mountain near Troy;★ the site of the beauty contest among the goddesses Pallas★ (Minerva), Venus,★ and Juno★ at which Paris★ awarded the prize to Venus★ because she promised to give him Helen★ as his wife.

Idmon   A prophet, one of the Argonauts.

Ilisos   A river in Attica.★

Ilium   Another name for Troy,★ derived from Ilus, the son of Tros (for whom Troy was named).

Iolcos   A city of Thessaly★ (Greece), modern Volos; home of Jason;★ port of departure for the *Argo.*★

Ionian   Asiatic or Athenian Greek, as opposed to mainland and particularly Peloponnesian (Mycenaean) Greek.

Isthmos   See Corinth.

Ithaca   An island in the Ionian Sea; home of Ulysses.★

Ixion   A mythical criminal who attempted to rape Juno★ but was tricked into making love to a phantom made of clouds instead. The off-spring of this union were the centaurs. Ixion's son, Pirithous,★ attempted to rape Proserpina,★ wife of Dis★ and goddess of the dead.

Jason   Son of Aeson;★ husband of Medea;★ commander of the *Argo.*★

Juno   Wife and sister of Jupiter;★ patron of Argos★ and of Jason.★

Jupiter   Most powerful of the gods; lord of the thunderbolt; ancestor of the Cretan house of Minos.★

Laertes   Father of Ulysses.★

Laomedon   Father of Priam;★ cheated Neptune★ and Phoebus★ of their wages for building Troy;★ also cheated Hercules★ of his promised reward for saving Laomedon's daughter; as a consequence, Hercules attacked and captured Troy.

Lerna   (1) Home of the Hydra.★ (2) Fountain near Corinth.★

Lesbos   An Aegean island plundered by Achilles★ before the Trojan War.

Lesser Bear   See Arctus.

Lethe   The river of forgetting; one of the rivers of the underworld.

Leucate   An island in the Ionian Sea.

Libra   The zodiacal sign Libra.

Libya   General term for North Africa.

Lucifer   The "Bringer of Light," the morning star.

Lucina   The "Bringer to Light," goddess of childbirth.

Lycaon   "Wolfman." Arcadian king, father of Callisto★; changed into a wolf by Jupiter★ because he killed a human being as a sacrificial offering.

Lynceus   An Argonaut famous for his ability to see great distances.

Lyrnesos   A town in the vicinity of Troy.★

maenad   A woman "possessed" or maddened by the power of a god (usually Bacchus)* and endowed with superhuman strength and subhuman ferocity.

Maeotis   The Sea of Azov and its environs.

Malea   A headland in the southern Peloponnesus (Greece).

Marathon   A coastal area of eastern Attica;* home of a fierce bull killed by Theseus.*

Mars   God of war; lover of Venus.* See Gradivus.

Meander   The Meander (now the Menderes) River, in Asia Minor (Turkey).

Medea   Daughter of Aeetes,* king of Colchis;* wife of Jason;* stepmother of Theseus.*

Medes   Inhabitants of Parthia* (ancient Iran).

Medusa   A deadly female monster whose hideous face turned anyone who saw her into stone; killed by the hero Perseus.

Megaera   See Erinys.

Meleager   See Althea.

Memnon   Son of Aurora (Dawn), the last ally to come to Troy's* aid; killed by Achilles* before the eyes of his mother and his uncle (Priam).*

Menelaus   King of Sparta;* son of Atreus;* brother of Agamemnon;* husband of Helen.*

Minos   King of Crete; father of Phaedra* and Ariadne.*

Minyae   (1) The people of the Minyius River, in Greece. (2) The Argonauts.

Molossians   People of Epirus famous for their dogs, "Dalmatians."

Mopsopia   Athens.

Mopsus   A prophet; one of the Argonauts.

Mothone   A town at the foot of Mount Pelion,* in Thessaly* (Greece); ruled by Philoctetes, whose bow (inherited from Hercules)* the Greeks needed to procure the fall of Troy.*

Mycenae   A town near Argos;* home of Agamemnon.*

Mysia   See Telephus.

naiads   Female water spirits (nymphs).

Nauplius   An Argonaut; later lured a Greek fleet to shipwreck because of his anger at the Greeks for their mistreatment of his son Palamedes.

Neptune   God of the (Aegean) sea, of horses, and of earthquakes; father of Theseus* (Aegeus,* who is Theseus' father in some versions, is himself essentially "the Aegean"); one of the gods who built Troy.*

Nereids   Female sea deities (nymphs); daughters of Nereus.*

Nereus   A lesser sea god; father of the Nereids* and of Thetis,* thus grandfather of Achilles.*

Neritos   An island near Ithaca* in the Ionian* Sea.

Nessus   A centaur (see Ixion) who attempted to rape Deianira, a wife of Hercules.* Hercules killed him with a poisoned arrow, but to gain revenge before he died Nessus gave Deianira some of his poisoned blood, which he said would help her restore Hercules' love if he was ever unfaithful to her. Hercules was unfaithful, and he was given a cloak, tainted with Nessus' blood which caused him to die in agony.

Nestor   The oldest Greek warrior in the Trojan War. His home was Pylos,★ in the western Peloponnesus (Greece).

Niobe   A Theban princess who angered Phoebus★ and Diana★ by boasting that her children were more beautiful than they. As punishment, the two deities shot down all fourteen of Niobe's children with arrows, and she wept until she was turned to stone.

Notos   The southwest wind.

Nysa   A mountain, supposedly in India, associated with Bacchus.★

Oceanus   (1) A mythical river that flows round the world. (2) The Atlantic Ocean.

Oeta   A mountain in Thessaly★ (Greece), where Hercules★ died.

Oileus   An Argonaut; father of one of the two warriors named Ajax★ who fought at Troy.★

Olenus   A Greek town near modern Patras.

Ophiuchus   A constellation, now divided into two: the Snake Holder and the Snake.

Orestes   Son of Agamemnon.★

Orpheus   A Thracian singer, son of the Muse Camena,★ whose songs could beguile even trees and stones to move; an Argonaut. He was killed by maenads★ in Thrace:★ his head was torn off and it floated down the river Hebrus★ into the Aegean and across to Lesbos.★

Pallas   A goddess identified with Minerva (Athena); builder of the *Argo.*★ Pallas' citadel = the acropolis of Athens.

Pan(s)   Goat god(s), pursuers of (and pursued by) dryads.★

Pangaeus Mountain   A mountain in Thrace,★ near Philippi.

Paris   Son of Priam★ and Hecuba;★ abductor of Helen.★ See Ida.

Parnes   A mountain range in Attica.★

Parnethus   An area between Attica★ and Boeotia.

Paros   An Aegean island famous for its marble.

Parthia(ns)   An Iranian people, who became dominant in Persia about 250 B.C.

Pasiphae   Daughter of Sol★ (the Sun); wife of Minos;★ lover of a bull by whom she became mother of the Minotaur (see Daedalus); also mother of Phaedra,★ Ariadne,★ and Androgeos.

Patroclus   A close companion of Achilles★ at Troy.★ When Achilles would not fight because of his quarrel with Agamemnon,★ Patroclus was permitted to put on Achilles' armor and fight in his place. He was thus the "false Achilles." Hector★ killed him.

Pegasus   (1) A horse with wings, born from the blood of the dying gorgon Medusa.★ (2) The constellation Pegasus.

Pelasgians   Aboriginal, non-Greek-speaking inhabitants of Greece.

Peleus   Son of Aeacus,★ often associated with Mount Pelion,★ in Thessaly★ (Greece). Peleus killed his brother Phocus, then traveled to Phthia,★ where he was cleansed of bloodguilt but accidentally killed his purifier. In exile at Iolcus,★ he was again purified (by Acastus,★ son of Pelias).★ He was rewarded for his courage by being given Thetis★ as his bride. She bore him Achilles.★

Pelias   Uncle of Jason★ who usurped power at Iolcus★ and sent Jason on his quest for the Golden Fleece; killed unintentionally by his daughters, who dismembered and cooked him in the mistaken belief that they could rejuvenate him with Medea's★ spells and potions.

Pelion   A mountain in Thessaly★ (Greece).

Pelops   Son of Tantalus;★ father of Atreus;★ grandfather of Agamemnon★ and Menelaus;★ killed and dismembered by his father to provide a banquet for Jupiter★ but later restored to life. The Peloponnesus ("Island of Pelops") was thought to be named for him. Thus "Pelopian" often means "Peloponnesian" or "Corinthian," as Corinth★ guards the entrance to the Peloponnesus.

Pelorus   The northeast coast of Sicily, associated with Scylla.★

Penthesilea   Queen of the Amazons★ who led an army against the Greeks at Troy★ and was killed by Achilles.★

Peparethos   A small island off the coast of Thessaly★ (Greece).

Pergamum   The citadel of Troy.★

Periclymenus   Son of Neptune★ who could change shape; an Argonaut; killed by Hercules★ while he was in the form of a fly.

Perseis   Wife of Sol★ (the Sun); mother of Aeetes,★ king of Colchis;★ grandmother of Medea.★

Phaedra   Daughter of Minos★ and Pasiphae.★

Phaethon   Son of Sol★ (the Sun). Having persuaded his father to let him drive the solar chariot for a day, Phaethon lost control of the horses, caused great damage in heaven and on earth, and was finally struck by a thunderbolt from Jupiter.★ His body fell into the mythical river Eridanus. His sisters, who came there to mourn him were metamorphosed into trees, and their tears became amber.

Pharis   A small town near Sparta★ (Greece).

Phasis   The river Rioni★ (now in the Soviet Union), on which Medea's★ city, Colchis,★ was situated.

Pherae   A city in Thessaly★ (Greece); home of Admetus★ and Alcestis.★

Philoctetes   See Mothone.

Phlegethon   A fiery river of the underworld.

Phlyeis   A region of Attica.★

Phoebe   Goddess of the moon; sister of Phoebus.★ See Diana.

Phoebus   A god famous for his beauty, his bow and arrows, and his love of music; identified with the daylight and Sol★ (the Sun) and also called Apollo; one of the gods who built Troy.★

Phrixus   Traveled on the golden-fleeced sheep with his sister Helle.★ Unlike Helle, he arrived safely in Colchis,★ his destination. See Helle.

Phrygia   The area of Asia Minor (Turkey) in which Troy★ was situated.

Phthia   A city in Thessaly★ (Greece) known for the ferocity of its inhabitants, notably Achilles.★

pietas   Dedication to one's gods, country, and family.

Pindus   A high mountain on the borders of Thessaly★ (Greece) and Epirus.

Pirene   A Corinthian fountain from which Tantalus★ drank.

Pirithous   Son of Ixion★ and friend of Theseus.★ He and Theseus went together into the underworld to carry off Proserpina,★ the wife of Dis.★

Pisa   A town in the Peloponnesus (Greece); = Olympia.

Pittheus   King of Troezen,★ in the Peloponnesus; father of Aethra, Theseus'★ mother.

Pleiades   (1) A cluster of stars in the constellation Taurus.★ (2) Daughters of Atlas, the mythical giant who holds up the skies.

Pleuron   A coastal town in Aetolia (Greece).

Pluto   See Dis.

Pollux   See Castor.

Polyxena   Daughter of Priam★ and Hecuba;★ sacrificed on the tomb of Achilles,★ near Troy,★ at the end of the Trojan War.

Pompey   A Roman politican and general of the first century B.C. who symbolized for many Romans the last days of freedom before the domination of the Caesars. He was defeated by Julius Caesar at Pharsalia, in Greece, in 48 B.C. and murdered in Egypt by a soldier named Achillas later in the same year. His body was left headless upon the seashore. Vergil in *Aeneid* 2.557 seems to be alluding to Pompey's death in his description of Priam's★ death, and Seneca seems to be echoing Vergil.

Pontus   The Black Sea area, including the Roman province of Pontus.

Priam   The last king of Troy★ and husband of Hecuba;★ he was twice left at the mercy of the Greeks when Troy was captured: first by Hercules,★ then by Agamemnon.★ Hercules spared his life; Pyrrhus,★ son of Achilles,★ murdered him on an altar. See Pompey.

Procrustes   A highwayman who lived near Eleusis;★ he mutilated and killed travelers by putting them on a short bed and lopping off their extremities if they were tall, or by putting them on a long bed and stretching them if they were small; killed by Theseus.★

Prometheus   A Titan★ who brought Jupiter's★ fire to mortals. For this offense he was chained to a crag on the Caucasus★ Mountain, where an eagle came daily to eat his liver. Each night the liver regrew; each day the eagle returned until Hercules★ killed it.

Proserpina   Daughter of Ceres,★ goddess of crops; abducted by Dis★ to be his wife among the dead. Pirithous★ attempted to carry her off from the underworld with Theseus'★ help.

Proteus   The Old Man of the Sea, a divine or semidivine being who could change into many shapes and was also a prophet. He lived off the coast of Egypt near the site of the famous lighthouse of Pharos, near Alexandria.

Prothoüs   A Greek leader in the Trojan War who came from the region of Mount Pelion,★ in Thessaly★ (Greece).

Pylos   See Nestor.

Pyrrha   "The Fiery One"; wife of Deucalion.★ After the Great Flood, she and Deucalion regenerated the human race by throwing stones over their shoulders: those thrown by Deucalion became men, those thrown by Pyrrha became women.

Pyrrhus   Son of Achilles★ and Deidamia (whom Achilles raped on the island of Scyros;)★ killer of Priam★ and symbol of Greek brutality during the destruction of Troy.★

Python   A snake which inhabited Mount Parnassus, in Greece, and which was killed by Phoebus★ (Apollo) before he set up his oracle at Delphi.

Rhesus   See Diomedes (1).

Rhipaean Mountains   A more or less mythical mountain range in central Europe beyond which the people especially loved by Phoebus,★ the Hyperboreans (those who live beyond Boreas,★ the north wind), supposedly lived in a kind of earthly paradise.

Rhoeteum   A headland jutting into the sea not far from Troy,★ and the town on that headland.

Rioni   The modern name of the river Phasis★ (in the USSR), on which Colchis,★ home of Medea,★ was situated.

Salamis   An island off the coast of Attica,★ in the Saronic Gulf.

Sarmatians   Nomadic Slavic people living in parts of what is now the western Soviet Union and part of Eastern Europe, between the Vistula and the Don; culturally related to the Scythians.★

Scarphe   A small town in central Greece.

Sciron's Rocks   Precipitous cliffs between Athens and Megara; named for the bandit Sciron, who kicked passers-by into the sea from them. Sciron was killed by Theseus.★

Scylla   A voracious female seamonster with many doglike heads who lay in wait for sailors. Her traditional site in the works of later Greek and Roman writers is off the Sicilian coast. See Pelorus.

Scyros   An island off the coast of Euboea (Greece), where Thetis★ hid Achilles★ from Greek recruiters who wanted him to fight at Troy.★ See Achilles.

Scythians   Nomadic people of eastern Europe and Asia whom the Romans knew mostly from contacts in the areas adjoining the Black Sea; rendered as "Cossacks" in the translation. See Sarmatians.

Seres   The Chinese.

Sidonian   (1) Of Sidon in Phoenicia (modern Lebanon), or of a city colonized by the Phoenicians, such as Carthage (in Tunis) or Thebes★ (in Greece). (2) Colored with the crimson murex dye for which the Phoenicians were famous.

Sigeum   A town near Rhoeteum★ and Troy,★ in Asia Minor (Turkey).

Sinis   A bandit who lived on the Isthmus of Corinth.★ He tied passing travelers between two bent pine trees, which he then released; when the trees sprang apart, the victim was torn in half. He was killed by Theseus.★

Sinon   A Greek spy who persuaded the Trojans to take the Wooden Horse into Troy.

Sirens   Mermaid-like singers whose beautiful voices lured sailors to destruction. Enchanted by the Sirens' song and eager to find its source, sailors were drawn off course to a shore where they crashed on treacherous rocks.

Sisyphus   Son of Aeolus★; king of Corinth★, famous for his ability to tell lies; condemned after death to roll a stone up a mountainside forever in retribution for his crimes.

Sol   The (god of the) Sun. See Phoebus.

Sparta   A city in the Peloponnesus.

Stymphalian birds   Mythical birds whose feathers were lethal shafts; killed by Hercules.★

Styx   (1) An allegedly poisonous river in the Peloponnesus. (2) The most famous of the rivers of the dead in Greco-Roman myth. An oath sworn by the Styx was binding even on the gods.

Suebians   A Germanic tribe living east of the Elbe and known for its practice of human sacrifice.

Sunion   A promontory on the coast of Attica.★ It was here, in some versions of the myth, that Aegeus★ kept watch for the return of his son Theseus★ from Crete and the Minotaur. When Aegeus saw the black sails of the returning ship (Theseus had forgotten to change them), he assumed his son was dead and threw himself into the sea, thereafter known as the Aegean. A famous temple of Neptune★ (Poseidon) was later built on the promontory.

Symplegades   Mythical rocks in the sea which stood apart and separate until a moving object tried to pass between them, at which time they clashed together. The *Argo*★ had to sail through them. After its safe passage, the rocks remained apart and never clashed together again.

Syrtes   Traditionally treacherous shallows off the coast of Tunis, in the Gulf of Sidra.

Taenarum   A cave in the southern Peloponnesus through which Hercules★ dragged Cerberus★ out of the underworld; one of the traditional entrances/exits of the underworld. See Avernus.

Talthybius   A Greek messenger. In the manuscripts he is the messenger only for the appearance of Achilles'★ ghost in *Trojan Women*, but it makes sense to give him the lines simply marked *nuntius*, "messenger," too.

Tanais   The Don River.

Tantalus   A king of Lydia (in Asia Minor [Turkey]); the son of Jupiter;★ a wealthy and criminal ruler who sacrificed and cooked his own son, Pelops,★ as a banquet for the gods. For his sins Tantalus was punished in one of two ways, according to various authors: (1) He was imprisoned in the underworld, where he was forced to stand in flowing water up to his neck, with grape clusters hanging above his head. Whenever he reached up to eat or down to drink, the grapes and the water receded beyond his reach. (2) He was left in constant fear of a stone poised over his head, forever about to fall. His daughter was Niobe.★

Tartarus   The deepest pit of the underworld, where the most terrible criminals are punished; it was guarded by the dog Cerberus.★

Taurus   A mountain range running inland from Lycia, in southwest Turkey. In Latin the name is suggestive of *taurus*, "bull," and the zodiacal sign Taurus.

Taygetus   A mountain range near Sparta.★

Telemachus   Son of Ulysses.★

Telephus   Son of Hercules★ and Auge, the daughter of a king of Arcadia★ (Greece); he eventually became king of Mysia,★ in Asia Minor (Turkey). His city was attacked by Achilles★ and the Greeks, who mistook it for Troy,★ and Telephus was wounded by Achilles. The only (and paradoxical) cure for the wound proved to be the rust from the spear that had wounded him. (Thus Pyrrhus★ can claim that Achilles' weapons cure as well as kill.)

Tempe   A valley in Thessaly★ (Greece).

Tenedos   An island off the coast of Troy,★ plundered by Achilles.★

Tethys   Wife of Oceanus;★ mother of Thetis,★ and thus grandmother of Achilles.★ If Ceres★ is a kind of Mother Earth, Tethys is a kind of Mother Ocean.

Teucer   Father of Dardanus★ and ultimate ancestor of the Trojan royal house.

Thebes   (1) A city of Boeotia (Greece), founded by a Phoenician explorer and exile, Cadmus; home of the prophet and Argonaut Mopsus.★ (2) A city in Asia Minor, home of Andromache.★

Thermodon   A river near the Black Sea, best known for its associations with the Amazons.★

Theseus   Son of Neptune★ or Aegeus;★ stepson of Medea;★ famous as a killer of monsters in and around Attica★ (see Marathon; Procrustes; Sciron's Rocks; Sinis). Later he went to Crete, where he killed the Minotaur. He left Crete with Ariadne,★ daughter of Minos,★ but abandoned her on the island of Naxos. On his return to Athens he neglected to change the black sails on his ship, and Aegeus,★ interpreting them as a sign of his son's death, committed suicide (see Sunion). Theseus fought and defeated the Amazons★ and married their queen, Antiope,★ by whom he had a son, Hippolytus.★ He later married Ariadne's sister, Phaedra.★ Theseus is often treated by ancient writers as a semihistorical figure (as in Plutarch's *Lives*, where, as founder of the Athenian state, he is paired with the legendary founder of Rome, Romulus).

Thessaly A region of north-central Greece, in which Jason's★ hometown of Iolcos★ is situated. Thessaly is also famous as the home of Achilles,★ who was born and raised there by the centaur Chiron.★ It is no less famous for its horses (and centaurs), and for its magic and witches. For many Roman writers, Thessaly is also ominous as the site of the battle of Pharsalia (48 B.C.), where Julius Caesar defeated the republican armies under Pompey.★

Thetis Mother of Achilles★ and wife of Peleus.★

Thrace A mountainous and barbaric area in what is now the border regions of Greece, Bulgaria, and Turkey. Its northern boundary was the river Danube, and it was bisected by the river Haemus.★ In Seneca's day only the part south of the Haemus was, strictly speaking, Thrace. The northern area was the province of Moesia. Thrace was the home of Orpheus.★

Thria A lowland community in western Attica,★ near Eleusis.★

Thule Probably Iceland.

Thyestes See Atreus.

Tigris A river running through present-day Turkey and Iraq; for all practical purposes, the easternmost limit of Roman influence in Seneca's day.

Tiphys The helmsman of the *Argo*.★

Titan (1) Sol★ (the Sun). (2) One of a family of giants who ruled the earth until their defeat by Jupiter★ and the Olympians, who imprisoned them under Mount Aetna.★

Titaressos A river in Thessaly★ (Greece) which flows into the river Peneus. Seneca seems to think it flows into the Aegean.

Tityos A son of Earth who attempted to rape Leto, the mother of Phoebus★ (Apollo) and Diana.★ He was punished in the underworld by having his ever-regenerating liver eaten by two vultures.

Tonans The Thunderer (Jupiter).★

Trachis A town in central Greece under the control of Achilles'★ family.

Tricce A town in Thessaly★ (Greece).

Triptolemus A hero of Eleusis,★ linked with the cult of Ceres★ and Proserpina.★

Tritons Minor (and musical) sea divinites.

Troezen   A town on the east coast of the Peloponnesus.

Troy   A city on the Hellespont, twice conquered by the Greeks: first under Hercules,★ who was angered by the bad faith of its king, Laomedon,★ and then, in the next generation (when Laomedon's son Priam★ was king), by Agamemnon★ and a coalition of Greek leaders. The conquest was precipitated by the abduction of the Greek queen Helen,★ wife of Agamemnon's brother Menelaus,★ by Paris,★ son of Priam. Roman writers felt a special sympathy for the Trojans in their wars with the Greeks because of the tradition that Troy's founders originally came from Italy and that the Romans could trace their own ethnic origins to a refugee (Aeneas) who escaped from the second and catastrophic defeat of Troy by the Greeks (see Venus). It was rumored in the last half of the first century B.C. that Rome's Caesars intended to transfer the capital of the empire to a rebuilt Troy.

Tyndareus   King of Sparta;★ in some versions, father of Helen★ and her sister Clytemnestra, and of Castor★ and Pollux.★ Helen is often referred to as "daughter of Tyndareus."

Typhoeus   A monstrous, hundred-headed son of Earth who fought against Jupiter★ for control of the heavens; defeated and buried under Mount Aetna.★

Tyre   A city of Phoenicia (Lebanon), famous for its high living and its crimson dyes. See Sidonian.

Ulysses   Son of Laertes;★ the Roman Odysseus, generally treated unfavorably in Latin poetry because of his treacherous behavior, but presented as an exemplar of the suffering hero, worthy of comparison with Cato and Socrates, in Roman prose. The contrast is particularly sharp in Seneca: the Ulysses of *Trojan Women* is one of ancient tragedy's most villainous characters, but the Ulysses of Seneca's prose works is the embodiment of Stoic virtue.

Venus   Beautiful but faithless goddess of love; wife of Vulcan★ and lover of Mars;★ mother of Amor★ (Cupid)★ and, in Roman tradition, divine forebear of the Caesars because of their mythical descent from Aeneas, Venus' son by Anchises, a Trojan prince. In Latin the word *venus* often means essentially sexuality, even the sexual act.

Vulcan   The smelter of metals (Mulciber, in Latin); god of metalworking and fire, associated with volcanoes, especially Mount Aetna;★ husband of Venus.★

Xanthus   The main river in the vicinity of Troy.★

Zacynthos   An Ionian★ island near Cephallenia★ and Ithaca.★

Zephyr   The west wind; wind of springtime.

Zetes   See Boreas; Calais.

Library of Congress Cataloging-in-Publication Data

Seneca, Lucius Annaeus, ca. 4 B.C.–65 A.D.
  Phaedra.

  (Masters of Latin literature)
  Translation of: Phaedra.
  1. Phaedra (Greek mythology)—Drama.   I.   Ahl, Frederick
M.   II. Title.   III. Series.
PA6666.P5A45   1986   872'.01   86-47634
ISBN 0-8014-9433-8 (alk. paper)